To Ira,
I hope this brings back some great memories from your days growing up in Chicago. Enjoy!
Best Wishes
Mark Stang
9/18/01

1929 Chicago Cubs

Manager Joe McCarthy (standing, far left) and his team doff their caps for photographers as they open training camp on Catalina Island in 1929.

CUBS Collection

100 Years of Chicago Cubs Images

by

Mark Stang

ORANGE FRAZER PRESS
Wilmington, Ohio

ISBN: 1–882203–76–3

Copyright © 2001 by Mark M. Stang

Orange Frazer Press, Inc.

Box 214

37 ½ West Main Street

Wilmington, Ohio 45177

Telephone 1.800.852.9332 for price and shipping information

Web Site: www.orangefrazer.com

E-mail address: editor@orangefrazer.com

Library of Congress Cataloging-in-Publication Data

Stang, Mark (Mark Michael)
    Cubs collection : 100 years of Chicago Cubs images / by Mark Stang.
    p. cm.
    Includes index.
    ISBN 1–882203–76–3
    1. Chicago Cubs (Baseball team)--Pictorial works. 2. Baseball players--United
States--Portraits. I. Title

GV875.C6 S83 2001
796.357'64'0977311–dc21

                                                                2001037447

Printed in Canada

In 1908, the Chicago Cubs blew by their greatest rival, the New York Giants, to win a third straight National League pennant. The Cubs' infield played with precision and the names of Joe Tinker, Johnny Evers and Frank Chance became synonymous with the spectacular double play. The cadence of their names became part of the vocabulary after columnist Franklin P. Adams, a suffering Giants fan, penned this verse for the *New York Globe* on July 10, 1908.

Baseball's Sad Lexicon

By Franklin P. Adams

These are the saddest of possible words,

Tinker to Evers to Chance.

Trio of bearcubs and fleeter than birds,

Tinker to Evers to Chance.

Thoughtlessly pricking our gonfalon bubble,

Making a Giant hit into a double,

Words that are weighty with nothing but trouble,

Tinker to Evers to Chance.

Introduction

In the faces on these pages reside the images, legends and lore of Chicago Cubs baseball in the 20th century. Some of the photographs have brief tales to tell; other pictures, as the old saying goes, are worth a thousand words.

A few of the images are familiar, but many have never been seen before or were published only once, long ago. The 225 images in this book represent what I believe to be the best photographs held in 16 public and private collections.

I chose these photos for a variety of reasons. Some were obvious choices. A book covering 100 years of Chicago Cubs images couldn't omit Tinker, Hartnett, Banks or Sandberg. But beyond the Hall of Fame-caliber players, there are dozens of forgotten personalities whose stories and images are just as compelling.

When uncovering the activities of players like Hack Miller, both on and off the field, or the accomplishments of Jack Taylor and Jake Weimer, I knew they had to be included. Some behind-the-scenes personalities, such as owners, managers and broadcasters, also provided fascinating stories. When woven together, I sought to paint a picture that did justice to the rich tapestry that has been the tradition of Cubs baseball.

I see myself as a baseball archeologist, uncovering photographic treasures hidden for decades in dusty old files. The opportunity to bring a long forgotten photo back to life makes my search a rewarding one. I hope you will agree.

This book brings together the famous, the not-so-famous and the long forgotten personalities in Cubs history. It is not meant to be the 200 greatest players in Chicago Cubs history. Nor is it meant to be the greatest moments in Cubs history or a history of baseball in Chicago. There are other books on these topics.

So I now present to you the obvious and the obscure, the famous and the forgotten personalities of the last hundred years in Chicago Cubs history.

Mark Stang
2001

Acknowledgments

This project would not have been posssible without the assistance of many individuals. I was given complete access to the photo and clip files at *The Sporting News* in St. Louis. Archivists Steve Gietschier and Jim Meier were their usual helpful selves. Sincere thanks to Tim Wiles and Pat Kelly (and their staffs) at the National Baseball Library in Cooperstown for their assistance.

I am deeply indebted to several professional photographers whose work appears in these pages. Doug McWilliams, George Brace, Don Sparks and Skip Trombetti all provided key images. In addition, the Chicago Sports Photographers made available dozens of superb photos.

Vintage photo collectors Dan Knoll, Dennis Goldstein, Mike Mumby, Bill Loughman and Steve Blank graciously shared their troves of treasured images with me and Cubs fans everywhere. Mark Rucker at Transcendental Graphics filled in some of the gaps.

My thanks to archivist Leigh Moran at the Chicago Historical Society's *Chicago Daily News* negative collection for her cooperation in tracking down the final elusive shots. William Barrow at Cleveland State University made the defunct *Cleveland Press* photo files available. And Librarian Ray Zwick at *The Cincinnati Enquirer* helped, as well.

A deep debt of gratitude is owed Rosemary Goudreau for her tireless editing of the text. My thanks also to Phil Wood for his thorough fact-checking. Thanks also to Elaine Olund of Lamson Design for the original cover concept. Thanks to Monte Pietrosky and his staff at Litho-Craft in Cincinnati for their assistance with the photo imaging.

The format used in *Cubs Collection* owes it inspiration to a 1999 book I co-authored with Greg Rhodes entitled: *Reds in Black and White, 100 Years of Cincinnati Reds Images.* That book owes a debt of gratitude to the classic work by Neal and Constance McCabe, *Baseball's Golden Age: The Photographs of Charles Martin Conlon* (published in 1993).

Finally, the behind-the-scenes star, as always, is Ryan Asher. His technical wizardry and tireless dedication to providing the best possible image is evident on every page. Ryan also executed the page layout and the cover design.

To all these folks, I offer my sincere appreciation for their hard work and cooperation in making this project possible.

Frank Chance
First baseman, 1898-1912

At the start of the 20th Century, Chicago's National League team wasn't called the Cubs, didn't play at Wrigley Field and hadn't finished higher than third place in 10 years. Rather, the team was called the Colts, played at the West Side Grounds and drew small crowds grown accustomed to the team's losing ways.

On the bench sat a back-up catcher from California, Frank Leroy Chance. He was 22, but injury-prone and unimpressive behind the plate. Yet he showed promise with the bat and was exceptionally fast. Late in the 1902 season, he was given the chance to play first base — a move of historic proportions. The move teamed Chance with shortstop Joe Tinker and second baseman Johnny Evers, two rookies from the minors. Sportswriters dubbed the team "the Cubs" because of all the young players. Tinker, Evers and Chance formed the cornerstone of a Cubs dynasty that ruled the National League for the next eight years.

Playing every day, Chance led the league in 1903 with 67 stolen bases and batted .327. Chance was named captain because of his aggressive play and leadership on the field. He led the Cubs to 93 wins and a second-place finish, the team's best showing in a dozen years.

Chance was nicknamed "Husk" because of his physique. Still, he was quick. He stole 400 bases, a team record that stands today. He had a commanding presence and was known to physically threaten anyone who challenged his authority. But his win-at-all-costs attitude came at a price. He became the frequent target of beanballs and was hit in the head so often that he suffered severe headaches and increasing deafness. During one double-header in 1904, he was hit five times, finishing the day with a black eye and a lacerated scalp.

Midway through the 1905 season, with the team stuck in fourth place, Chance was named manager. His teammates lit up under his leadership and won 40 of their last 63 games. The spirit spilled over into 1906, when Chance led the Cubs to a record 116 wins and only 36 losses. Chance's ascension heralded a new era for Chicago sports fans and brought forth a dynasty that would deliver four National League pennants over the next five years.

Joe Tinker
Shortstop, 1902-1912; 1916

Joe Tinker was a graceful fielder known more for his defensive skills than his power at the plate. Growing up in Kansas, he worked as a plasterer and played semi-pro baseball on the weekends. After three seasons in the minors, he was signed by Chicago and became the starting shortstop in 1902. Although he was quick, Tinker had a tough start. He led the National League in errors his first season.

Late in the 1902 season, when a rookie second baseman named Johnny Evers joined the club, Tinker's troubles turned around. It was immediately apparent that Tinker and Evers clicked on the field. With a new-found confidence, Tinker played batters deep, knowing he could count on Evers to make the catch at second. Soon, the duo became one of the league's top defensive tandems.

But they fought constantly, often about perceived slights, and in 1912, their final season together, they had to be separated by teammates during a fight in the dugout during a game at Brooklyn.

Although quick with the glove, Tinker had a reputation as a weak hitter. Only once in his Cubs career did he bat over .290. He did, however, possess an uncanny ability to hit one of the game's most dominant pitchers, Hall of Famer Christy Mathewson of the rival New York Giants. His triple off Mathewson in the one-game playoff of the 1908 season sent the Cubs on a return trip to the World Series. Always a better hitter in clutch situations, Tinker was the first Cub to hit a home run in the World Series.

Besides his gifted defensive play, Tinker's greatest strengths were his ability to move baserunners along and his speed on the basepaths. He stole 304 bases with the Cubs and ranks fifth on the team's all-time list.

Johnny Evers
Second baseman, 1902-1913

At five-foot-nine and 125 pounds, Johnny Evers may have been one of the smallest men ever to have played in the major leagues. But Evers never let size stand in the way. He was a skilled defensive second baseman, part of the legendary infield trio of Tinker, Evers and Chance immortalized in Franklin P. Adams' classic poem. Evers was exceptionally quick, stealing 324 bases over his career, including 21 thefts of home. And he was unusually argumentative with umpires, players and managers. He was nicknamed, "The Crab."

Evers was a student of the game, often retiring to his hotel room with a copy of the official baseball rule book. His knowledge of the game's rules led to one of baseball's strangest plays, forever immortalized as "the Merkle Boner."

It happened at New York's Polo Grounds on September 23, 1908. The Cubs were playing the New York Giants, their rivals in a heated pennant race. The game was tied 1-1 in the bottom of the ninth inning. The Giants had runners on first and third base. Giants batter Al Bridwell hit a single, allowing the runner on third to head home for the win. Amid the celebration that broke out, Evers shouted for his teammates to throw him the ball. Evers knew that the baserunner on first, Fred Merkle, never tagged second base. He had simply headed for the clubhouse, believing the game over. With the crowd surging onto the field, Evers tagged second and notified Umpire Hank O'Day, who ruled Merkle out on a force play, negating the winning run. The game ended in a tie. Both teams protested to National League President Harry Pulliam who ruled that if the season ended with two teams tied for first place, a one-game playoff should decide the NL pennant. The Cubs traveled to New York and won the playoff game, securing their third straight World Series appearance.

Giants fans forever blamed Fred Merkle for losing the pennant. But in the story of the Cubs' win, it was Johnny Evers' mastery of the rule book that brought victory.

Jack Taylor
Pitcher, 1898-1903; 1906-1907

For a four-time 20-game winner, pitcher Jack Taylor has been all but forgotten, perhaps because scandal seemed to follow his wake.

Chicago purchased Taylor's contract in September 1898 after he won 28 games for Milwaukee. In Chicago, Taylor won all five of his starts, each a complete game, starting one of the most remarkable streaks ever achieved by a major-league pitcher. Over a ten-year career, Taylor started 286 games and completed 278 of them. He was a workhorse of the pitching staff, twice throwing more than 350 innings in a season.

His best season was 1902 when he went 22-11, threw eight shutouts and led the National League with a 1.33 ERA. Included in his wins: a 19-inning game he completed against Pittsburgh, winners of the NL pennant that year.

But the following year, Taylor was touched by scandal. Chicago owner James Hart accused him of deliberately losing a pre-season exhibition game against the cross-town rival White Sox. The charges were never proven, but Taylor's relationship with the club was irreparably damaged. Although he won another 21 games for the Cubs in 1904, Taylor was traded to the St. Louis Cardinals in return for a young pitcher with one year of major-league experience, Mordecai "3 Finger" Brown. It proved a turning point in the fortunes of the Chicago franchise. Brown would be the ace of the Cubs' young staff for the next decade.

In St. Louis, Taylor continued to excel, winning 21 games and leading the league with 39 complete games in 1904. But again, he was accused of deliberately throwing an exhibition game. In July 1906, Taylor was traded back to the Cubs. He went 12-3 for the second half of the year, again achieving 20 victories in a season. In 1907, Taylor managed only six wins for Chicago and was released. He spent the next six seasons in the minors before retiring after the 1913 season. Taylor died in 1938 at age 65.

Johnny Kling
Catcher, 1900-1908; 1910-1911

Johnny Kling was a superb defensive catcher and anchor of the Cubs dynasty that won the National League pennant in 1906, 1907 and 1908. After two years as a part-time player, Kling became the everyday catcher in 1903. His emergence as a regular allowed Frank Chance to move to first base. Possessing a rifle arm, Kling was famous for throwing out baserunners. He also had a reputation for constantly chattering at opposing batters, earning him the nickname "Noisy."

Following the championship season of 1908, Kling went to see Cubs owner Charles Murphy about a pay raise. Murphy refused, so Kling sat out the entire 1909 season. He went home to Kansas City, where he operated a pool hall and had a few other business interests. When the Cubs failed to win a fourth straight pennant in 1909, many observers said the team missed Kling and his handling of the pitching staff. Kling returned for the 1910 season and the Cubs once again found themselves atop the National League standings at season's end. But Murphy held a grudge and traded the 35-year old Kling to the Boston Braves early in the 1911 season. There, he managed for one year in 1912, before retiring after a final season with Cincinnati.

In retirement, Kling was a successful businessman. His investments in Kansas City real estate holdings, which included two hotels, made him a wealthy man. In 1934, at the height of the Depression, he purchased the minor-league Kansas City Blues baseball team. Three years later, he sold the team to the New York Yankees for a handsome profit. Kling died in 1947 at age 71.

Jake Weimer
Pitcher, 1903-1905

Jacob Weimer's overpowering fastball earned him the nickname "Tornado Jake." The 29-year-old rookie left-hander dazzled National League hitters with his speed. In 1903, he won 21 games. The next year, he won another 20 games, recorded five shutouts and was the toast of the league. Newspaper reporters sang his praises and compared him to legendary New York Giants pitcher Christy Mathewson. Pittsburgh owner Barney Dreyfuss, whose team won the 1903 pennant, offered Chicago $12,500 for Weimer's contract. It was an enormous sum at a time when the average player earned less than $3,000 a season. When news of the offer hit the Chicago papers, fans expressed outrage and demanded that the club turn Dreyfuss down flat. The outpouring kept Weimer in Chicago for one more season, where he won another 18 games.

By 1906, Chicago was desperate to find a veteran third baseman to compliment the Tinker, Evers and Chance infield, so Weimer was dealt to Cincinnati for Harry Steinfeldt. It was a trade that benefitted both clubs, as Weimer again won 20 games for the Reds.

After three seasons in Cincinnati, Weimer was 35 years old and his skills had diminished. He retired to work in the Chicago stockyards and died in 1928.

Jimmy Slagle
Outfielder, 1902-1908

Nicknamed "Shorty," Jimmy Slagle, the Cubs' starting centerfielder and lead-off hitter, took utmost advantage of his small stature. Slagle once recalled: "I was only 5'6" and batted left-handed and when I crouched over the plate, there wasn't much for a pitcher to throw at. In fact, I used to walk so often that one of our pitchers once said I was the only player he ever saw who stole first base."

Slagle's first year with the Cubs was his best. He batted .315 and stole 40 bases, both career highs. In the 1907 World Series, Slagle stole six bases, a record that stood for 60 years until Lou Brock stole seven in 1967. An arm injury shortened Slagle's career and after two seasons in the minors, he retired after the 1910 season.

Carl Lundgren
Pitcher, 1902-1909

Pitcher Carl Lundgren went straight from the University of Illinois to the Chicago Cubs without spending a single day in the minor leagues. It probably helped that he'd recently pitched the Fighting Illini to two Big Ten titles in 1900 and 1902.

With the Cubs, Lundgren won 17 games in 1904 and again in 1906, but saved his best for the championship season of 1907. Lundgren won 18 games, threw seven shutouts and had an ERA of 1.17. It is a tribute to the excellence of the other Cubs pitchers that, despite all of his success, Lundgren was never chosen to pitch in any of the Cubs' World Series appearances.

In 1908, Lundgren suddenly lost his effectiveness. He won only six games and early in the 1909 season, was released by the Cubs. After two partial seasons in the minors, Carl Lundgren returned to collegiate baseball in 1912 as head coach at Princeton. But it was in the Big Ten conference that Lundgren had his greatest success as a coach. Starting in 1918, his Michigan teams won three straight titles. And after returning to the University of Illinois, he made it five straight with titles in 1921 and 1922. His Illinois teams won four more Big Ten titles before his premature death of a heart attack in 1934 at age 56.

Bob Wicker
Pitcher, 1903-1906

Bob Wicker pitched the Cubs' first nine-inning no-hitter of the 20th Century.

It was June 11, 1904, and the Cubs were playing the New York Giants at the Polo Grounds in New York. More than 38,000 fans packed the ballpark, the largest crowd ever to attend a game at the time. Wicker was matched against the Giants' ace, "Iron Man" Joe McGinnity, who the previous year had won 31 games and pitched an astounding 434 innings — the all-time record by a pitcher in the 20th Century. McGinnity was seeking his 13th consecutive win and was pitching superbly, blanking the Cubs through nine innings. Wicker was even better, holding the Giants hitless for nine innings before allowing a hit in the tenth. Wicker eventually won the game, 1-0 in 12 innings.

Wicker won 52 games for Chicago in just over three seasons. But in 1906, after winning just three of his first 10 starts, he was traded to the Cincinnati Reds for pitcher Orval Overall. He later spent several seasons pitching in the minor leagues before managing Spokane in 1915. Wicker died in 1955 at age 78.

"Big Ed" Reulbach
Pitcher, 1905-1913

Ed Reulbach pitched the only double-header shutout in the history of Major League Baseball.

Reulbach pitched two complete games against the Brooklyn Dodgers on Sept. 26, 1908, and allowed just eight hits, winning 5-0 and 3-0. It was the centerpiece of four consecutive shutouts that Reulbach would hurl in a season that saw him win 24 games.

The big right-hander, whose best pitch was a devastating curveball, was unusually durable. In 1905, his rookie season, Reulbach twice won games of 18 and 20 innings by identical 2-1 scores. In 1909, he put together a 14-game winning streak. Despite all his success, Reulbach was overshadowed in Chicago by teammate "Three Finger" Brown and White Sox pitcher "Big Ed" Walsh, making him the Windy City's third-best pitcher and its second "Big Ed."

Reulbach's one-hitter in Game 2 of the 1906 World Series held the major-league postseason record until Yankee pitcher Don Larsen threw a perfect game in 1956. Reulbach ranks third all-time among Cubs pitchers with 31 career shutouts.

Following a slow start in 1913, Reulbach was traded to Brooklyn. He later spent two seasons in the upstart Federal League, winning 20 games for Newark in 1915. After two final seasons with the Boston Braves, he retired. He died in 1961 at age 78.

Pat Moran
Catcher, 1906-1909

Pat Moran is best known as a manager who twice led teams to the World Series. As a Cubs player, he spent most of his time on the bench, playing second string to catcher Johnny Kling.

During his days in the dugout, Moran studied the opposition and became known for his ability to steal the other team's signs. He also became known for his expertise in handling a pitching staff. When he was traded to the Phillies after the 1909 season, Moran tutored rookie pitcher Grover Cleveland Alexander, who led the league with 27 wins in 1911.

In his first year as Phillies manager in 1915, Moran brought home a National League pennant for the team that had finished sixth the year before. After four seasons, Moran became manager in Cincinnati and in his first year with his new team, again won a pennant. Moran died of liver disease during spring training of 1924. Those close to him blamed it on his daily consumption of bootleg liquor during Prohibition. Moran was 48.

Arthur "Solly" Hofman
Outfielder, 1904-1912; 1916

"Solly" Hofman was the Cubs' all-around player during their greatest era. His ability to play every position except pitcher and catcher made him indispensable to Manager Frank Chance.

Hofman may be best remembered for the trick catches he made in the Cubs' outfield, where he earned the nickname "Circus Solly." Fans flocked to pre-game warmups to watch his acrobatic catches. Cubs teammate Lefty Leifield recalled, "He'd dive, somersault and catch balls sensationally in all parts of the outfield. One of his favorite stunts was to catch the ball behind his back. His sleight-of-hand tricks with a baseball during the warm-ups before the game always brought out the crowd early to watch him perform."

Hofman was traded to Pittsburgh during the 1912 season. He later played two seasons in the Federal League before briefly returning to the Cubs to finish out his career in 1916.

Mordecai "Three Finger" Brown
Pitcher, 1904-1913; 1916

Mordecai Peter Centennial Brown overcame a childhood injury to become one of baseball's greatest pitchers.

At age seven, Brown caught his hand in a corn grinder on his uncle's Indiana farm. He lost his index finger and mangled the two middle fingers on his right hand. But he never gave up the dream to play baseball. He worked in the coal fields, but spent his free time playing third base for a local semi-pro team. When the team's pitcher injured his arm, Brown took his place. To everyone's amazement, Brown's deformed grip allowed him to throw a deadly sinkerball that tailed away from opposing batters.

After winning 50 games in two minor-league seasons, Brown was signed by the St. Louis Cardinals at age 26. He won just nine games for the lowly Cardinals, but caught the eye of Cubs manager Frank Selee in 1903. The next year, the Cubs sent their best pitcher, two-time 20-game winner Jack Taylor, to the Cardinals in return for Brown. Cubs fans were outraged, but the deal proved fortuitous. Taylor won 21 games for St. Louis in 1904, but his best days were over. Brown was just coming into his own. In 1906, he won 26 games, threw ten shutouts and led the National League with a 1.04 ERA. It was the first of six straight seasons with 20-plus victories.

"Three Finger" Brown's pitching hand
c. 1915

Mordecai Brown's right hand was the subject of great curiosity as sports fans and photographers sought the source of his pitching success.

The nation's sportswriters dubbed him "Three Finger," although his teammates preferred "Miner" or "Brownie." When asked by a sportswriter whether pitching without an index finger was a disadvantage, Brown replied, "I don't know. I've never done it the other way." Unlike other pitchers who used their thumb and index finger to apply pressure to the ball, Brown spun his pitches off his middle finger, which caused them to sink and fade away from the batter. Hitters found themselves harmlessly pounding his pitches into the ground for outs. Brown's 1906 season was one of the greatest ever. He went 26-6, threw 10 shutouts and had an ERA of 1.04.

So great was Brown's pitching dominance that in his nine seasons with the Cubs, his ERA exceeded 1.90 only three times. His career ERA of 2.06 is third on baseball's all-time list.

Charles W. Murphy
Owner, 1905-1915

Charles Webb Murphy owned the Cubs during their greatest era.

Murphy was a reporter for *The Cincinnati Enquirer* at the turn of the century. He later became sports editor of a rival paper headed by Charles Taft, brother of future President William Howard Taft. When Murphy learned that the Chicago franchise was up for sale, he persuaded Charles Taft to loan him the money to buy the team. He convinced Taft that he could turn the Cubs franchise into a gold mine — and he was right.

With a nucleus of great players in place, the Cubs won a record 116 games in 1906, taking the first of three straight trips to the World Series. Attendance at the West Side Grounds soared and Murphy was able to repay the $100,000 loan to Taft in just 12 months. The combination of Murphy's financial resources and Manager Frank Chance's ability to scout talent proved unbeatable. The team acquired key players in trades and dominated the National League for five years.

But the duo's relationship suffered when the Cubs finished second in 1911 and 1912. Murphy began questioning Chance's abilities as manager. Chance sold his 10 percent share in the Cubs to outside interests and Murphy fired him after the 1912 season. Murphy chose Johnny Evers to manage the 1913 season, but fired him after one year. In three years, Murphy had three different managers. His frustration with the team's fall in the standings led him to sell the Cubs in 1915. He retired a millionaire and invested in a series of movie houses throughout the Midwest. Murphy died in 1931 at age 63.

Jack Pfiester
Pitcher, 1906-1911

Jack Pfiester was a left-hander with a nasty curveball who signed with the Cubs at age 27, having twice won 20-plus games for Omaha.

His first year in Chicago, Pfiester went 20-8 and became the Cubs' best weapon against the rival New York Giants. Pfiester's dominance of New York earned him the nickname "Jack the Giant Killer." In six seasons, Pfiester compiled a 15-5 record against the Giants, including seven shutouts. In 1907, he led the National League with a 1.15 ERA. However, Pfiester didn't enjoy the same success in the postseason. His best effort ended in a loss to the White Sox in Game 3 of the 1906 Series, despite allowing just four hits. His lone World Series victory came in Game 2 of the 1907 Series over the Detroit Tigers.

Arm trouble shortened Pfiester's career and he was released after the 1911 season. After two partial seasons in the minor leagues, he retired to a farm outside of Cincinnati. Pfiester died in 1953 at age 75.

Orval Overall
Pitcher, 1906-1910; 1913

Orval Overall was one of the most dominant pitchers of his era, even though his major league career lasted only seven seasons.

A collegiate all-star at the University of California, Overall began his career with the Tacoma Tigers of the Pacific Coast League earning $300 a month, a large sum for those days. In 1904, he won 32 games in less than a year. Cincinnati purchased his contract in 1905 and in his debut season with the Reds, Overall won 17 games.

Cubs manager Frank Chance, a fellow Californian who had played against Overall in the offseason, recommended the Cubs trade for the big right-hander. In 1906, the Cubs sent pitcher Bob Wicker and $2,000 to the Reds for Overall. The move gave the Cubs the league's most dominant pitching staff as Overall joined Reulbach, Pfiester, Lundgren and "Three Finger" Brown.

In 1907, Overall won 23 games and led the league with eight shutouts. He was chosen to start Game 1 of the World Series against Detroit, which ended due to darkness in a 3-3 tie after 12 innings. Three days later, Overall held the Tigers to five hits and won, 6-1. The Cubs had won four straight games, giving them their first championship in more than 20 years.

The following season, Overall won 15 games but saved his best for the postseason. He threw complete game victories in Games 2 and 5 of the World Series, holding the Tigers to five hits in 18 innings. The Cubs won their second straight world championship.

In 1909, Overall again won 20 games and led the league in strikeouts and shutouts. It would be almost 60 years before another Cubs pitcher, Ferguson Jenkins, matched his 205 strikeouts in a single season.

When his victories slipped to 12 in 1910, Cubs owner Charles Murphy cut Overall's salary. Rather than take it, the pitcher retired to California. After sitting out two seasons, Overall attempted a comeback with the Cubs in 1913, but his touch was gone. He won just four of nine starts and was released to pitch briefly in the Pacific Coast League before retiring for good. He later entered the banking business in California. Overall died in 1947 at age 66.

Jimmy Sheckard
Outfielder, 1906-1912

Samuel James Sheckard played his first major league game at age 19, but didn't join the Cubs until nine seasons later. By the time he came to Chicago in 1906, Sheckard had led the National League in stolen bases twice; home runs and triples once each.

Considered one of the league's best defensive outfielders, Sheckard's career was almost cut short by a freak accident in 1908. After turning his ankle while sliding into third base, a teammate urged Sheckard to apply a home remedy to reduce the swelling. Attempting to remove the cap from a bottle of ammonia, the bottle exploded and Sheckard was blinded by the spray. Rushed to a nearby hospital, it took days before doctors knew whether he would regain his sight. Although he missed more than a month, Sheckard recovered to play another four seasons in left field for the Cubs. In 1911 and 1912, he led the National League in walks. In 1913, the Cubs sold Sheckard to the Cardinals and he retired after one season.

He returned to Pennsylvania and worked for a dairy. Later, he operated a filling station. In 1947, at age 68, Sheckard was struck and killed by a car while walking to work

Harry Steinfeldt
Third Baseman, 1906-1910

Third baseman Harry Steinfeldt was an eight-year veteran when the Cubs chose him to round out the legendary infield of Tinker, Evers and Chance.

Steinfeldt played for Cincinnati, but the Reds badly needed pitchers and so in 1906, agreed to trade Steinfeldt to the Cubs for pitcher Jake Wiemer, who'd twice won 20 games.

Once in Chicago, Steinfeldt had the best year of his career. He batted .327 and led the league in hits and RBI. His defense led the league and he added 29 stolen bases for good measure. He played with the Cubs until the end of the 1910 season, when an undisclosed illness slowed him up. He signed with Boston, but didn't last the season.

It is only due to the cadence of Franklin P. Adam's legendary poem that Tinker, Evers and Chance were immortalized and not Harry Steinfeldt. In 1914, three years after he retired, Steinfeldt died of paralysis at the age of 36.

Henry "Heinie" Zimmerman
Infielder, 1907-1916

Henry Zimmerman was a rough-and-tumble player whose sixth season with the Cubs ranks as one of the greatest in National League history.

In 1912, Zimmerman won the equivalent of the league's Triple Crown, awarded to the player who leads the league in home runs, RBI and batting average. It was a feat so rare that in the entire 20th Century, only four players won the Triple Crown in the National League.

That year, Zimmerman collected 207 hits and added 14 home runs and 103 RBI, while batting .372 to finish atop the standings in all three offensive categories. For added measure, he stole 23 bases and his 41 doubles also led the league.

But for all his accomplishments on the field, it was Zimmerman's off-field behavior that generated the headlines. He was constantly fined by manager Frank Chance for breaking training rules, a euphemism for drunken behavior. He was a regular holdout at contract time and constantly fought with opposing players and managers.

Despite twice leading the league in RBI, the Cubs traded Zimmerman to the Giants midway through the 1916 season rather than agree to his contract demands. Zimmerman's behavior problems continued after the trade. In 1917, he was fined for cursing and throwing a ball at an umpire. In 1919, he was accused of offering bribes to his Giants teammates to throw games during the final Cubs-Giants series of the season. Zimmerman was suspended from organized baseball and never played in the majors again.

In 1935, back in Chicago, Zimmerman was named in a federal indictment for tax evasion charges filed against noted gangster "Dutch" Schultz, with whom he jointly owned a speakeasy during Prohibition.

Frank Chance
Manager, 1905-1912

There were more senior players, but Frank Chance was named manager of the Cubs at age 27 because he was the team's natural leader, evidenced by his on-field play and off-field demeanor.

Chance earned the players' respect because he played hard and he played hurt. He suffered severe headaches from taking so many pitches to the head. When his players failed to go all out, Chance enforced his will through fines and physical intimidation. He expected nothing less than aggression from his opponents, too. After a baserunner landed on his foot in a game against Pittsburgh, Pirates outfielder "Chief" Wilson told Chance, "I hope you're not hurt." After limping back to the dugout, Chance told his players that Wilson would never play for the Cubs. "He should have said, 'I hope you lose your leg the next time.'"

Another time, during a game in New York, Chance charged into the stands after a fan threw a pop bottle and hit him in the head. Chance ran down the man and beat him, challenging onlookers to interfere.

While Chance was known for aggressiveness, his ability to judge talent proved his greatest contribution to the Cubs' success. He made trades for players who helped mold the team into a dynasty. He offered veterans for unproven youngsters, often against the wishes of the fans. But eventually, he developed a club that sportswriters deemed "a team without a weakness." His 1906 team won 116 games, a feat unequaled in baseball history. His Cubs won four National League pennants in five seasons and twice won the World Series. Sportswriters dubbed Chance "the Peerless Leader."

A growing dispute with owner Charles Murphy led Chance to leave the Cubs after the 1912 season. He would later manage the New York Highlanders (the Yankees' predecessor) for two seasons. But so great was his reputation in Chicago that when he returned as manager of the visiting team in 1913, Chicago fans honored him with "Frank Chance Day" at Comiskey Park. Temporary bleachers were erected to accommodate the record crowd. The Governor of Illinois and the Mayor of Chicago both presided.

Late in the 1914 season, Chance returned to his native California to tend to his real estate holdings. Lured out of retirement in 1923 to manage the Boston Red Sox, he resigned after a single season when the team finished last.

Johnny Evers
Second Baseman, 1902-1913
Manager, 1913; 1921

Johnny Evers' career was marked by phenomenal success and recurring tragedy.

Evers and Joe Tinker were immortalized in Franklin P. Adam's poem as baseball's first double-play tandem, but in reality, they didn't turn any more double plays than any other duo in the National League. They did, however, lead the league in one category: silence. Evers later recalled, "We didn't even say hello for at least two years. We went through two World Series without a single word. And I'll tell you why. It was early in 1907, he (Tinker) threw me a hard ball. It wasn't any farther than ten feet away. And the ball broke my finger. I yelled at him, `You so and so.' He laughed. That's the last word we had. Tinker and myself hated each other, but we loved the Cubs. We wouldn't fight for each other, but we'd come close to killing people for our team. That was one of the answers to the Cubs' success."

Evers missed almost the entire 1911 season after suffering a nervous breakdown following the death of his good friend, a sportswriter for a local paper. The reporter died in a car accident in which Evers was driving. About that same time, Evers also learned that his business partner back home in Troy, New York, had gambled away his life savings at the local racetrack and had skipped town.

Evers was named manager of the Cubs when Frank Chance left after the 1912 season. But the team had gotten older and most of its star players were long gone. Despite a third-place finish, Evers was released after just one season. He signed with the Boston Braves and was the star on the 1914 "Miracle Braves," a team that came from nowhere to defeat Connie Mack's highly favored Philadelphia Athletics in the World Series. But it was Evers' last season as an everyday player.

In 1917, Evers retired at age 36. In 1921, he returned to Chicago as manager of the Cubs, but he was fired before the season ended. Evers returned to upstate New York where he spent the last five years of his life in a hospital bed partially paralyzed from a stroke. He was elected to the Hall of Fame in 1946, along with Tinker and Chance. He died the following year at age 65.

Joe Tinker
Shortstop, 1902-1912; 1916
Manager, 1916

When Johnny Evers was named Cubs manager in 1913, he traded his old double-play partner, Joe Tinker, to Cincinnati. For one season, Tinker was player-manager of the Reds and hit .317, but the Reds finished seventh and Tinker fought with Reds owner Garry Hermann.

Tinker returned to Chicago in 1914 as player-manager of the Federal League franchise, the Chicago Whales. The new league had successfully raided National League rosters by offering fatter contracts and Tinker's Whales included several of his former Cubs teammates. The Whales were a strong team, finishing second in 1914 and first in 1915. But financial losses caused the owners of the Federal League to disband after only two seasons.

Still, Tinker's name was big box office in Chicago and so the owners of the Cubs asked him to manage the team in 1916. When the Cubs won only 67 games and finished fifth, Tinker was replaced. Starting in 1917, Tinker spent the next four years running the minor league franchise in Columbus, Ohio. In 1922, he moved to Orlando, Florida, and purchased the club there.

Sadness seemed to follow Tinker in retirement. His first wife committed suicide in 1923. He made, then lost, a fortune in the Florida real estate boom. He bounced from job to job, even ran a saloon for a few years. His health grew poor. He had diabetes and lost his left leg to complications from the disease.

Tinker was elected to the Hall of Fame in 1946. He died two years later on his 68th birthday.

Tinker Field in Orlando is named in his honor.

Leonard "King" Cole
Pitcher, 1909-1912

For one brief moment, Leonard Leslie Cole was the talk of the National League.

The Cubs brought Cole to Chicago at the end of the 1909 season after just one season of Class D ball. In his first start, the 23-year old threw a complete-game shutout and the Cubs signed him on the spot.

The next year, the tall right-hander had the best winning percentage in the National League. Cole went 20-4, threw four shutouts and helped the Cubs win their fourth pennant in five years. In the 1910 World Series against the Philadelphia Athletics, Cole outdueled Hall of Famer "Chief" Bender in Game 4 for the Cubs' only win of the Series.

But in 1911, although Cole won another 18 games, his mind wasn't always on the game. Manager Frank Chance repeatedly fined him for leaving the team, often for days at a time. Cole also disrupted the Cubs' train trips because of his chronic sleepwalking. After a poor start the next year, Cole was traded to Pittsburgh and shortly thereafter, sent to the minor leagues.

In 1913, Cole again attracted major-league suitors after throwing a no-hitter while pitching for Columbus, Ohio. His old boss, Frank Chance, manager of the New York Highlanders, outbid several teams and signed Cole. Cole won 11 games for the lowly Highlanders in 1914, but it was his last full year. He was diagnosed with cancer. Although he started several times in 1915, he soon retired to his home in Michigan, where he died six months later. "The King" was 29 years old.

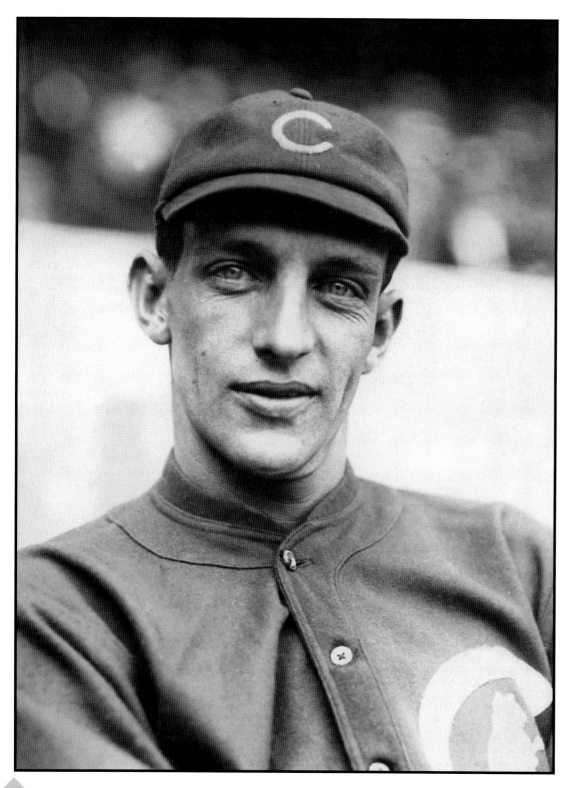

Frank "Wildfire" Schulte
Outfielder, 1904-1916

Frank Schulte was the first player to hit four grand slams in a year, a record that stood until 1955 when broken by another Cub, Ernie Banks.

Schulte almost missed the majors.

His father, a German immigrant and successful contractor, offered his 16-year old son $1,000, an enormous sum in those days, to give up the game. Frank decided to play semi-pro ball instead. The Cubs signed him three years later, almost by accident. A Cubs scout went to Syracuse to scout another player but wound up signing Schulte. His first year with the Cubs, Schulte hit .286 and was in the big leagues to stay.

Schulte became one of the game's premier sluggers. In 1910 and 1911, he led the league in home runs. In 1911, he batted .300, with 21 home runs and 121 RBI. He was voted the league's most valuable player. He was also a daring baserunner and his 22 career steals of home remain the Cubs' all-time record.

Schulte liked to have fun off-field, too. He liked to drink with a young *Tribune* sportswriter, Ring Lardner, who later used Schulte as the inspiration for his sports novels. Schulte also fancied himself an expert on thoroughbred racehorses. He even purchased one named "Wildfire," racing it at tracks around the country. Schulte was probably the only major leaguer to owe his nickname to a racehorse.

After patrolling right field for 11 years, Schulte was traded to Pittsburgh midway through the 1916 season. He spent two more years playing part-time, but then was done in the majors. He spent another five years managing in the minors before retiring for good in 1923. Schulte died in 1949 at age 67.

Jimmy Lavender
Pitcher, 1912-1916

Twice, spitballer Jimmy Lavender was the toast of Chicago: once for throwing a no-hitter and once for stopping a star pitcher's record-breaking winning streak.

In his first season with the Cubs, Lavender pitched against the New York Giants' Rube Marquard, who had a 19-game winning streak going, a record that stands today. The game was played at the West Side Grounds. Lavender's teammate, Jimmy Archer, recalled: "The ballpark was jammed. They were out to see Marquard win his 20th. When we walked into the park, you could have knocked us over with a feather. Even the ushers were pulling for Marquard and the Giants. I never saw anything like it. We were like strangers on a foreign field." The Cubs won, 7-2, and Marquard's string was snapped. "We went on to win," Archer recalled, "but as we walked off the field, our own fans were still yelling at us, `Yeah, you guys would have to go and do a thing like that.'"

In 1915, Lavender was even more dominant. On August 31, at the Polo Grounds, he threw a no-hitter against the Giants. Years later he recalled: "The closest thing to a hit in my no-hitter came on the last out of the game. John McGraw put in Eddie Grant to pinch-hit for the pitcher and he hit a liner that I thought sure was a goner. But Bob Fischer, our shortstop, pulled it down and came running in to give me the ball. They were hitting my spitter into the dirt."

Lavender was traded to the Phillies after the 1916 season, when he won only five games. He went home to Georgia, where he grew peaches. In 1922, at age 38, Lavender was lured out of retirement to pitch one final game for the minor league Atlanta Crackers. He lost, 2-0.

Lavender died in 1960 at age 75.

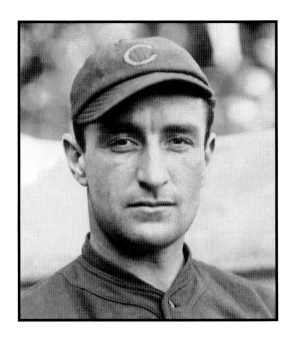

Jimmy Archer
Catcher, 1909-1917

Jimmy Archer became one of the National League's premier defensive catchers despite his unusual throwing style.

Archer liked to throw out baserunners from a crouch. Major-league managers said he'd have to learn to throw standing up or he'd never be successful, but Archer had a reason for his approach. His right arm was severely scarred in an accident as a teenager, when he was seared by boiling tar. When his arm finally healed, it was an inch shorter than it used to be. Archer found he could get the ball to base more quickly by throwing from the squatting position.

Archer paid a high price for his aggressive play behind the plate. He shattered a kneecap, broke an index finger four times and broke a collarbone once. Injuries shortened his career and after the 1917 season, his contract was sold. He played only half a season more.

In retirement, Archer worked as an inspector for the Armour meat packing company in Chicago. In 1931, he saved the lives of two truck drivers overcome by carbon monoxide fumes. Jimmy Archer died in 1958 at age 74.

Mordecai "Three Finger" Brown
1916

The Chicago Cubs and New York Giants had a great rivalry during the first decade of the 20th Century, highlighted by a duel between two future Hall of Fame pitchers — New York's Christy Mathewson and Chicago's Mordecai "Three Finger" Brown.

The two would face each other 24 times in their careers. Mathewson won four of the first five games, including a no-hitter in 1905. Over the next three years, Brown won nine straight, including a one-game playoff that decided the 1908 National League pennant.

The playoff game came about because of the infamous "Merkle's Boner" play that left the Cubs and Giants tied at season's end, forcing a one-game playoff to decide the NL pennant. The atmosphere on playoff day at the Polo Grounds was electric. An overflow crowd tried to force its way in by setting fire to the outfield fences. Policemen on horseback, others with fire hoses, had to force the crowd back.

Jack "The Giant Killer" Pfiester started, but Cubs manager Frank Chance pulled him after four of the Giants' first five batters reached base. Mordecai Brown came in with the Cubs trailing, 1-0. Brown retired the side and gave up only one run. He defeated Mathewson, 4-2, giving the Cubs their third consecutive NL pennant. In each of the Cubs three subsequent World Series appearances, Brown threw a shutout.

The pitching rivalry spanned 14 seasons and ended with Brown, 13; Mathewson, 11. Brown retired in 1916 after spending two years in the Federal League and a final few months back with the Cubs.

Brown is the club's all-time leader in shutouts with 48, and complete games with 206. He is second in wins with 188.

Brown died in 1948. A year later, he was elected to the Baseball Hall of Fame.

Albert "Lefty" Leifeld
Pitcher, 1912-1913

Before joining the Cubs in 1912, "Lefty" Leifeld was known as one of the Pittsburgh Pirates' best pitchers.

Fans would recall a game he pitched against the Cubs on July 4, 1906. Leifeld, in his second year with the Pirates, was matched against the Cubs' Mordecai "Three Finger" Brown, who would win 29 games that year. In a classic pitchers' duel, both allowed but one hit. Leifeld had a no-hitter entering the ninth inning, but allowed a single and lost the game, 1-0.

Leifeld was traded to the Cubs early in the 1912 season. He went 7-2 over the last half of the year, but unfortunately for Cubs fans, his arm went bad. He was sent to the minors after starting only one game in 1913. Leifeld returned to the big leagues four years later to pitch for the St. Louis Browns. He stayed three years before finally retiring in 1920.

Leifeld later coached for major and minor league clubs, but spent many more years working for the water department in St. Louis. He died in 1970 at age 87.

Roger Bresnahan
Catcher, 1900; 1913-1915
Manager, 1915

Roger Bresnahan's greatest fame came as catcher for Giants' pitching great Christy Mathewson. His greatest legacy is this: Bresnahan is credited with being the first catcher to wear shin guards.

Although Bresnahan started out on the mound, he was most effective behind the plate. Unusually quick for a catcher, Bresnahan twice stole more than 25 bases in a season. In 1907, Bresnahan debuted his shin guards, which were modeled after those worn by cricket players. They were bulky and Bresnahan was widely ridiculed by opposing players and fans as a sissy. But within two years, his innovation had become standard equipment around both leagues.

Bresnahan spent six years with the Giants before he became player-manager for the St. Louis Cardinals in 1909. Four years later, Bresnahan, no longer an everyday player, was signed by the Cubs to serve as catcher Jimmy Archer's backup. In 1915, Bresnahan was named Cubs manager, but a fourth-place finish and new owners led to his release after only one season.

Bresnahan purchased the minor league club in his hometown, Toledo, and ran it for eight years. He coached briefly in the majors, but wound up working as a salesman for the Buckeye Brewing Company in Toledo. Bresnahan died in 1944. He was elected to the Hall of Fame the next year.

Larry Cheney
Pitcher, 1911-1915

An injury to his pitching hand turned Larry Cheney into a 20-game winner in the majors.

The injury happened during his first start in the majors. Cheney was pitching for the Cubs against Brooklyn at the West Side Grounds when batter Zack Wheat hit a line drive that screamed back toward Cheney's head. Cheney remembered, "I just had time to throw my hand up to save my face." But the force of the ball drove his pitching hand into his nose, breaking both his thumb and nose. Cheney later recalled, "The next year, my thumb was so weak that I couldn't grip a ball with it. So I developed an overhanded delivery. Believe it or not, my overhanded pitch didn't break down, it shot up, a sort of rise ball." Armed with his new pitch, Cheney had the best season of his career in 1912. He won 26 games and led the league with 28 complete games.

The next season, he added a spitball to his pitching arsenal and again won 21 games. In 1914, Cheney won 20 games for a third year in a row. His success, however, came at a price. His trick pitches were hard for catchers to hold on to. Cheney led the league in wild pitches six times in his career, setting the Cubs' single-season record with 26. In addition, Cheney became the workhorse of the Cubs' pitching staff, throwing 300-plus innings for three straight seasons.

Cheney started slowly in 1915 and was traded to Brooklyn mid-season. He won 18 games for the pennant-winning Dodgers in 1918, but his best days were behind him. By 1919, at age 33, he was washed up. Cheney pitched in the minors for three more years before retiring to Florida to oversee his orange groves. He died in 1969 at age 82.

Mr. and Mrs. Frank Chance
California, c. 1914

California was home to Frank Chance and the Cubs' famed manager invested his earnings wisely. He purchased real estate and invested in oil wells near Long Beach. In 1908, Cubs minority owner Charles Taft rewarded Chance for a sensational game-winning play by allowing him to purchase 10 percent of the Cubs for $10,000.

In 1912, Chance sold his shares for $140,000 and was promptly fired by owner Charles Murphy. When he was lured to New York to manage the Highlanders in 1913, Chance signed a three-year contract at a hefty salary and was given 5 percent of the net profit as a bonus.

But Chance's name was still box-office in Chicago and in 1924, White Sox owner Charles Comiskey signed him to manage his team. But that spring, Chance took ill and never left California. He died that fall at age 47.

Newspaper reports valued his estate at nearly $300,000, an incredible sum for a ballplayer to have amassed. In 1946, Chance was reunited with Tinker and Evers when all three were elected to the Hall of Fame.

Vic Saier
First baseman, 1911-1917

Vic Saier replaced "peerless leader" Frank Chance when age and injuries caught up with the renowned Cubs first baseman.

Saier was an average batsman, but stole 20 or more bases in three seasons. In 1913, he led the National League in triples with 21. And he holds the distinction of having hit five home runs off Hall-of-Fame pitcher Christy Mathewson, more than any other player. Saier's career was cut short when he broke his leg early in the 1917 season. He tried a comeback with the Pirates in 1919, but at age 28, he was through in the majors.

James "Hippo" Vaughn
Pitcher, 1913-1921

"Hippo" Vaughn became one of the game's most dominant left-handers, five times winning 20 or more games for the Chicago Cubs. But his talent wasn't immediately apparent.

The big Texan was wild in his early days. The Highlanders and Senators both gave up on him and sent him back to the minors after four years. But that is where he finally learned to harness his fastball. Vaughn won 14 games for Kansas City in 1913 and the Cubs acquired him late that season.

In 1914, Vaughn won a club-best 21 games for the Cubs. Soon, he became the team's workhorse, pitching more than 290 innings six times. In the seven seasons between 1914 and 1920, Vaughn won 143 games for Chicago.

His best season was 1918. Vaughn won 22 games and led the National League in wins, ERA, strikeouts and shutouts, with eight. Vaughn started and completed three games for the Cubs in the 1918 World Series against the Boston Red Sox, allowing only three runs in 27 innings. Despite an ERA of 1.00, he lost two of the games. A young Red Sox pitcher named Babe Ruth won Game 1, 1-0. Vaughn lost Game 2 to Carl Mays, 2-1. But Vaughn shut out the Red Sox in Game 5, 3-0.

For all his success, "Hippo" Vaughn is best remembered for a game he lost. On May 2, 1917, at Wrigley Field, Vaughn faced the Cincinnati Reds. Neither Vaughn nor Reds pitcher Fred Toney allowed a hit for nine innings. In the top of the tenth inning, the Reds finally scored and Vaughn lost the game, 1-0. It was the only nine-inning double no-hitter in major league history.

By 1921, Vaughn had a sore arm and at age 33, he accepted a lucrative offer to pitch for a semi-pro team in Beloit, Wisconsin. After another 12 seasons, Vaughn retired for good in 1934. He died in 1966 at age 78.

Fred "Cy" Williams
Outfielder, 1912-1917

"Cy" Williams was dealt to the Phillies in the Cubs' second-worst trade ever. Only the 1964 trade of outfielder Lou Brock to the Cardinals was worse.

Williams proved to be a late bloomer. By age 29, he had hit only 34 home runs in six seasons with the Cubs. But after leaving Chicago, Williams became one of the National League's premier home-run hitters. Over the next 12 years, he hit 217 home runs for the Phillies. A dead pull-hitter, he took advantage of the short right-field fence at his home field, the Baker Bowl. "Williams was the most consistent dead-right-field hitter I ever saw," Reds manager Bill McKechnie once said. Williams said, "I couldn't hit a ball to left field if my life depended on it." To defend against him, opposing managers would shift their players to the right of second base, leaving open third base and left field. It was the first "Williams Shift." The second came against Red Sox slugger Ted Williams two decades later.

Williams led the National League in home runs three times. He tied Babe Ruth for the most home runs in the majors in 1923, with 41. He batted over .300 six times, including 1926, when he hit .345 at age 38.

Williams retired after the 1930 season. He moved to Wisconsin and worked as an architect, putting his degree from Notre Dame to use. He died in 1974 at age 86.

Grover Cleveland Alexander
Spring Training, 1918

Baseball's future was uncertain when the United States entered World War I in 1917. Club owners lost most of their star players to military service and ballpark attendance dropped sharply. To cut costs, owners decided to shorten the 1918 regular season.

Before spring training, Phillies owner William Baker, always short of cash, decided to sell his brightest star rather than risk losing him to the draft. He figured the owners of the Chicago Cubs had plenty of money and desire, given that it had been eight long seasons since their last trip to the World Series.

At age 30, Phillies pitcher Grover Cleveland Alexander was coming off three spectacular seasons. He had won 30-plus games each of the last three years. And he'd led the National League in wins, ERA, complete games, strikeouts, shutouts and innings pitched.

The Cubs gave Baker $55,000 and two players for Alexander and his catcher, Bill Killefer. That spring, Alexander trained with his new team in California, but pitched only three games for the Cubs before he was notified to report for military duty. He joined an artillery unit and was shipped to the front lines in France. The thunder of the unit's big guns left Alexander deaf in one ear and suffering from epilepsy. When he returned to the States in the spring of 1919, he was in no shape to pitch.

Claude Hendrix
Pitcher, 1916-1920

Claude Hendrix twice won 20 games in a season, but he is best remembered for the way his career ended.

Hendrix joined the Pittsburgh Pirates as a 22-year-old in 1911. The next year, he went 24-9 and had the best winning percentage in the National League. After one more season with the Pirates, Hendrix was lured to the newly formed Federal League. He joined player-manager Joe Tinker's Chicago Whales and was the league's top winner, with a 29-11 record. When the Federal League disbanded after only two years, the owner of the Whales bought controlling interest in the Cubs. He signed the Whales' best players to new contracts and moved the Cubs to his newly built ballpark at the corner of Clark and Addison Streets. Hendrix' best season with his new team would be in 1918. He won 19 games and helped pitch the Cubs to the World Series. The big right-hander was also an excellent hitter and his managers often used him as a pinch-hitter in key situations.

But during the 1920 season, allegations surfaced that Hendrix wagered heavily against the Cubs in a game he was scheduled to pitch against the Phillies. Word reached Cub officials, who pulled Hendrix just before the game started. Hendrix denied the charges, but a grand jury was convened. It was no secret among baseball's owners that players were wagering on games, sometimes even offering to throw a game in an effort to supplement their meager salaries. The testimony of several players led to allegations of fixed games in both leagues. Eventually, the grand jury heard testimony about the "fixing" of the 1919 World Series between the cross-town Chicago White Sox and the Cincinnati Reds. The club owners hired judge Kennesaw Mountain Landis as baseball's first commissioner and charged him with cleaning up baseball's tarnished image. Landis' inquiry led to the lifetime ban of eight White Sox players, including Shoeless Joe Jackson.

At age 30, Hendrix's career was over. Baseball owners refused to offer him a contract. He never pitched in the major leagues again. Hendrix retired to Allentown, Pennsylvania, and operated a cafe until his death in 1944 at age 54.

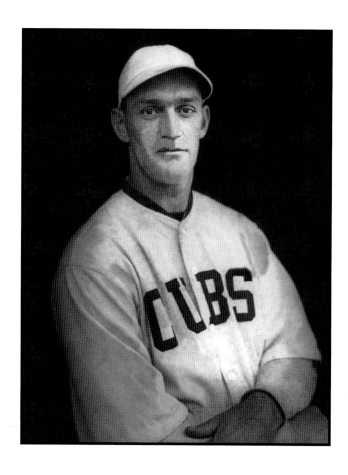

George "Lefty" Tyler
Pitcher, 1918-1921

Eight-year veteran "Lefty" Tyler had the best year of his career after arriving in Chicago in 1918. He won 19 games, including eight shutouts and one marathon game.

Tyler pitched the longest complete game in Cubs history on July 17, throwing 21 innings and defeating the Phillies, 2-1. In the 1918 World Series against the Boston Red Sox, Tyler started three games. He won Game 2 by a score of 3-1, evening the series. In Game 4, he allowed two runs over seven innings and the Cubs lost, 3-2. In Game 6, the team lost 2-1 when a Cubs error allowed two unearned runs to score. His ERA for the series was 1.17.

Early in the 1919 season, Tyler developed lameness in his pitching shoulder. He attempted to pitch despite the pain, but after several starts was benched and missed almost the entire season. The Cubs management, eager for an explanation, sent Tyler to the Mayo Clinic. Doctors discovered that Tyler's problem was with his teeth and ordered all but two pulled. Tyler's shoulder problems disappeared and he was back pitching for the Cubs the next season, winning 11 games.

But it was his final season in the majors. Despite winning three of his first six starts in 1921, Tyler was sent to the minors. He never pitched in the majors again. He became a minor-league umpire and later worked for the New England Power Company in Boston. Tyler died in 1953 at age 63.

Charlie Hollocher
Shortstop, 1918-1924

Charlie Hollocher was a small man with immense talent, but his career was cut short by stomach ailments.

His first year with the Cubs, the 21-year-old Hollocher hit .316, stole 26 bases and led the National League in hits. Fans loved his hustle on defense and his numbers bore them out. Hollocher twice led the league's shortstops in fielding.

But in the middle of the 1920 season, Hollocher left the team without explanation. The Cubs found him in St. Louis, his hometown, complaining of severe stomach pains. The Cubs sent him to several doctors, but no one could find anything wrong. Hollocher returned to play for two more years. In 1922, he batted .340 and struck out only five times all season.

During spring training in 1923, he again left the team, complaining of stomach pains. Again he was sent to doctors. Again they could find no medical explanation. Hollocher was persuaded to return to the Cubs, and he batted .342 despite playing just half the season. But it was his final season. At age 28, Hollocher left the majors for good and returned to St. Louis. There, he held several jobs, including running a tavern. In 1940, continuing to suffer from severe stomach pains, Hollocher committed suicide. He was 44.

Fred Merkle
First baseman, 1917-1920

Fred Merkle's baserunning blunder stripped the 1908 New York Giants of a pennant win and forced the team into a one-game playoff with the Cubs. The Giants lost the playoff and the pennant. New York fans never forgot "the Merkle Boner."

A decade later, Merkle was playing for his old rivals, the Cubs. The team purchased him from the Brooklyn Dodgers in 1917. The Cubs needed someone to play first base because Vic Saier broke his leg six games into the season.

Always a solid hitter, Merkle led the Cubs with 65 RBI in 1918. But by 1920, he was no longer an everyday player. Merkle played in five World Series in his 16-year career, all on the losing team.

When Merkle retired, he moved to Florida.

In 1950, he reluctantly accepted the Giants' invitation to return to the Polo Grounds for an old-timers game. Merkle was wary of the reception he might receive, but when he was finally introduced, the crowd cheered loudly. He announced to assembled reporters: "I stayed away from New York for 23 years and I wasn't interested in even visiting here again. But it's strange how things work out. I never had such a good time." Merkle died in 1956.

Female Ushers
Wrigley Field, 1918

During World War I, the nation had a manpower shortage and women were needed to fill jobs in factories and offices. In Chicago, the Cubs hired women to be ushers at the ballpark. Here, young Beatrice Solomon (left) and Violet Flatow pose for a photographer during a game in July 1918.

William Wrigley, Jr.
Owner, 1919-1932

Businessman William Wrigley Jr. was a self-made multi-millionaire who used his personal fortune to transform the Cubs franchise into a consistent contender.

Wrigley started in Philadelphia, working as a door-to-door soap salesman for his father's company. He was a natural salesman and was determined to make a mark in business. In 1907, after migrating to Chicago and getting into the chewing gum business, Wrigley wagered his life savings on a risky strategy, a national advertising campaign. It cost nearly a million dollars, but Wrigley's brand of chewing gum became famous almost overnight. It made Wrigley a very wealthy man and allowed him to diversify his interests and time.

In 1916, Wrigley became a minority investor in the Cubs. The team was owned by a group of Chicago-area businessmen headed by Charles Weeghman, former owner of the city's Federal League franchise. Wrigley provided a steady flow of cash to the other investors and by 1919, was the club's largest single shareholder. In 1925, he bought out the remaining shares and assumed control of the Cubs.

Wrigley hired a local sportswriter, William Veeck, Sr., to run the club's day-to-day operations. He then set out to build other businesses, including a vacation resort at Catalina Island, located 22 miles off California's southern coast. Wrigley bought the island for $3 million, then built a luxury hotel, golf course and hundreds of bungalows to house the tourists he was sure would visit. He even operated a fleet of steamships to get people back and forth in comfort. To publicize his island paradise, Wrigley held a series of annual cross-channel swims and awarded the winner $25,000. He also decided the island would be the perfect home for the Cubs' spring training camp. And so beginning in 1921, with the exception of World War II, the Cubs held spring training at Catalina Island for the next 30 years.

Back in Chicago, Wrigley's investment in the team didn't immediately pay off, but the Cubs began moving up in the standings after Joe McCarthy arrived as manager in 1926. Wrigley gave Veeck and McCarthy the money to assemble a championship-caliber team, and in 1929, the Cubs won the pennant. While the stock market crash of 1929 tied the hands of most major-league owners, Wrigley's deep pockets rebuilt the Cubs' farm system, doubled Wrigley Field's seating capacity by adding a second deck and ensured a steady stream of fresh talent to keep the Cubs in the elite of the National League. But Wrigley lived to see only one pennant. In January 1932, William Wrigley, Jr., died at age 70.

Grover Cleveland Alexander
Pitcher, 1918-1926

Grover Cleveland Alexander's service in World War I changed him. It left him deaf in one ear, stricken with epilepsy and drinking heavily.

Before the war, playing with the Phillies, Alexander won 190 games in seven seasons, an average of 27 a year. But a year in the muddy trenches of France took its toll. When he returned, he was 30 and out of shape. It took him a year to regain his form, but when he was finally back, he was dominating. Alexander won 27 games and led the league in ERA and strikeouts in 1920. At one point, he won 11 games straight.

Alexander developed arm problems for the first time in the spring of 1921 and struggled through two mediocre seasons. But in 1923, he rebounded and won 22 games, his control never better. That year, he threw 52 consecutive innings without a walk. But the next spring, he fractured his wrist and missed half the season. And he continued to drink.

Alexander's drinking consumed him. To keep seizures at bay, he would sniff ammonia in the dugout between innings. But the ammonia made him look woozy on the mound. Determined to "take the cure," Alexander spent off-seasons in sanitariums trying to kick the habit, but he was never successful.

The arrival of Joe McCarthy as manager in 1926 spelled the end of Alexander's tenure with the Cubs. McCarthy expected his players to keep themselves in shape and he saw Alexander as a distraction to the Cubs' younger players. Alexander missed most of spring training with a broken ankle and disregarded orders to stop drinking. When his leg healed, Alexander often was in no condition to pitch. Midway through the season, McCarthy had seen enough. The Cubs put Alexander on waivers and the St. Louis Cardinals claimed him for $4,000.

Alexander was a big draw in St. Louis. An overflow crowd of more than 37,000 people jammed Sportsman's Park for his first game, which happened to be against the Cubs. They got to see Alexander take revenge against McCarthy by beating the Cubs 3-2 in 10 innings. Alexander won nine games that year for the Cardinals and helped them win the pennant. In the World Series, he was magnificent. He won Games 2 and 6 and in Game 7, he struck out the Yankees' Tony Lazzeri with the bases loaded to preserve the Cardinals' World Series victory by one run.

Alexander retired in 1930 at age 43. For the next 20 years, he drifted around the country, barnstormed briefly with the House of David team and held odd jobs. In 1937, he was elected to the Hall of Fame. He was there when the Hall was dedicated two years later. Still, he continued to drink. Alexander died broke and alone in 1950 at age 63.

William Veeck, Sr.
Executive, 1918-1933

William Veeck was a newspaperman given to grand plans for restoring the Cubs to their glory days.

Veeck was a sports columnist for *The Chicago American* who wrote under the byline Bill Bailey and gave candid assessments of the Cubs' shortcomings. In the spring of 1918, along with fellow sportswriters, Veeck was invited to a dinner at the home of Cubs owner William Wrigley. The group began to debate the Cubs' poor performance and Veeck had plenty to say. Wrigley asked whether Veeck thought that he could do a better job. Veeck reasoned that he couldn't do any worse. With that, Veeck quit his job at the paper and took a job in the Cubs' front office. The next year, he was named team president.

Veeck was an innovator. While the team was shaky, Veeck began to market the club and improve the bottom line. He offered the first Ladies Day promotion over the objections of rival club owners. Veeck figured that by letting women in once a week for free, he could build loyalty with a whole new segment of fans. In 1923, he convinced Wrigley to double the park's seating capacity by adding a second deck. And he allowed the Cubs' games to be broadcast on radio starting in 1925, a move highly criticized by other owners. The move proved a windfall because it widened the team's reach. Attendance at the ballpark soared.

Improving the club's performance on the field proved more difficult. When the team finished in last place in 1925, Veeck knew drastic measures were needed. He hired an unproven manager in Joe McCarthy, yet convinced Wrigley that the fastest way to win was to spend money on proven ballplayers. The Cubs purchased the game's premier second baseman, Rogers Hornsby, in 1929, and the team turned around, winning its first pennant in a decade. By 1932, the Cubs were champs again and remained one of the National League's dominant teams throughout the 1930's.

For his part, Veeck lived to see only two pennants won by the team he helped rebuild. In 1933, less than two years after the death of William Wrigley, William Veeck died of leukemia at the age of 55.

Bill Killefer
Catcher, 1918-1921
Manager, 1921-1925

Bill Killefer came to the Cubs because he was the catcher for Hall of Fame pitcher Grover Cleveland Alexander, who came to Chicago from the Phillies, where the two played together for 11 years.

Killefer was never a great hitter, and on the basepaths, he was called "Reindeer Bill" for his plodding style. But Killefer knew how to handle a pitching staff and he was a great tutor for rookie catcher Gabby Hartnett, who would become the best of an era. Because of his leadership style, the Cubs named Killefer manager when they fired Johnny Evers in 1921.

But in three years, the Cubs never managed better than a fourth-place finish. Midway through 1925, Killefer was released and replaced by Rabbit Maranville, who lasted two months. Killefer went on to coach with the Cardinals and in 1930, he was named manager of the St. Louis Browns. He later spent several years managing in the minors and as a scout for several major-league teams.

Cliff Heathcote
Outfielder, 1922-1930

Arnold "Jigger" Statz
Outfielder, 1922-1925

The Cardinals were in the middle of a doubleheader against the Cubs when St. Louis outfielder Cliff Heathcote learned he'd been traded to Chicago. "I was asleep on a trunk in the clubhouse," he later recalled, "when Branch Rickey, then manager of the Cards, awakened me and said, `You have on the wrong uniform and you're in the wrong clubhouse.'" Heathcote simply walked down the tunnel to the Cubs' clubhouse and joined his new team.

Heathcote became the Cubs' everyday right fielder and became especially popular among female fans. When he wasn't in the lineup, the front office was deluged with letters from women wanting to know why. Heathcote was noted for his basestealing exploits, once stealing home five times in a single season. Starting in 1927, his last four years with the Cubs were spent as the team's fourth outfielder, playing only against right-handed pitchers.

In 1931, Heathcote was waived to the Reds and retired the next year. In 1939, he died at the age of 40.

"Jigger" Statz spent 24 years as a professional ballplayer. Unfortunately for him, he spent 18 of those seasons in the minor leagues, the most by any player.

In 1919, the New York Giants signed Statz out of college but soon sent him to the minors. The Cubs acquired him in 1922 and made him a regular. Although he stood only five-foot-seven, Statz was an excellent defensive outfielder with a strong arm. His best season was 1923 when he batted .319, had 209 hits and scored 110 runs.

In 1925, Statz was sent back to the minors. In 1927, he spent his final two seasons in the majors with the Brooklyn Dodgers, before returning for another 14 seasons in the Pacific Coast League, where he made his mark. He was named the league's MVP in 1932 and, in 1934, he stole 61 bases at the age of 36. Statz ended his career as player-manager of the Los Angeles Angels. After retiring, he became a West Coast scout for the Cubs.

Charles "Gabby" Hartnett
Catcher, 1922-1940
Manager, 1938-1940

Charles "Gabby" Hartnett was the greatest catcher of his era in the National League.

The oldest child of a streetcar conductor, Hartnett became the Cubs' everyday catcher in 1924 and was quickly feared by baserunners around the league for his exceptional throwing arm. His constant chatter behind the plate earned him the nickname "Gabby." His aggressive handling of the pitching staff kept the Cubs hurlers focused on the game. And his batting average improved as his playing time increased. In 1924, he batted .299. The next year, he hit 24 home runs for the last-place Cubs.

In 1929, Hartnett suffered an arm injury in spring training and missed most of the season. But he rebounded in 1930 with the best year of his career, hitting .339. His 37 home runs and 122 RBI that year remain the Cubs' record for a catcher. In 1933, Hartnett was chosen to be the NL's starting catcher in the first All-Star game. It was the first of six All-Star appearances. When the Cubs won the 1935 pennant, Hartnett was voted the league's MVP.

In mid-season 1938, Hartnett became player-manager of the Cubs. In the final week of the season, his home run against the Pirates propelled the Cubs to their fourth World Series in 10 years.

But the next two years, the team slipped to fourth and fifth place. Hartnett was fired following the 1940 season. He went on to operate a bowling alley in suburban Chicago for many years. His last job in baseball was as a coach for the 1965 Kansas City Athletics. Gabby Hartnett was elected to the Hall of Fame in 1955. He died in 1973 on his 72nd birthday.

Lawrence "Hack" Miller
Outfielder, 1922-1925

"Hack" Miller was strong and liked to make a big first impression.

In his first year with the Cubs, Miller batted .352, the highest ever by a Cubs rookie. Mid-season, he hit two home runs and drove in six runs in the Cubs' 26-23 win over the Phillies. It was the highest scoring game in major league history.

Raised on Chicago's north side the son of a former circus strongman, Miller liked to show off his own strength. Crowds would gather when he would bend bridge spikes with his bare hands. He liked to amuse teammates in spring training by uprooting small trees on Catalina Island. And he once rescued a woman pinned beneath a touring car on a New York street. He simply lifted the car at one end, allowing the woman to be pulled free.

Miller's strength allowed him to use a 47-ounce bat, among the heaviest in the majors. But his massive build didn't help him run down fly balls in the outfield. After only two seasons, Miller was no longer an everyday player. Used mostly as a pinch-hitter, he was sent back to the minors early in 1925, where he continued to play for another four years. In retirement, Miller worked on the docks in the San Francisco Bay area.

Hal Totten
Broadcaster, 1925-1943

Pat Flanagan
Broadcaster, 1928-1943

The Chicago Cubs recognized the potential of radio early.

While rival owners feared radio broadcasts would eliminate the need to go to the ballpark, Cubs owner William Wrigley was certain the new medium would help him reach a bigger audience. And so in 1925, the Cubs began allowing their home games to be broadcast. Attendance soared. By the late 1920's, as many as five different stations carried Cubs games. Listeners could choose between Hal Totten at WMAQ, Pat Flanagan at WBBM and Quin Ryan at WGN, among others. By 1927, Totten was doing both the Cubs and White Sox games. He was later behind the mike for the first All-Star game in 1933 and for three World Series.

Flanagan was one of the first to re-create the Cubs' road games by using the Western Union teletype machine. Flanagan would sit in a studio in Chicago and announce road games by reading a pitch-by-pitch account relayed over the streaming ticker tape. Flanagan remained behind the Cubs' microphone for 16 seasons before giving way to Bert Wilson in 1944.

John "Sheriff" Blake
Pitcher, 1924-1931

"Sheriff" Blake is best remembered as the losing pitcher in Game 4 of the 1929 World Series.

The Cubs were playing the Philadelphia Athletics and were down, two games to one. In Game 4, the Cubs were leading 8-0 after six innings, but the pitching fell apart in the seventh. Before the inning was over, the Cubs were trailing 10-8. The starter was pulled, followed by three relievers, including Blake, who had entered the game when the score was tied, 8-8. Blake gave up singles to Jimmie Foxx and Al Simmons. He was replaced by Cubs pitcher Pat Malone, who gave up a double that allowed Foxx and Simmons to score, making Blake the losing pitcher. The Cubs never recovered and lost the Series in five games. Blake later recalled: "A friend of mine complained that he lost $10 when the Athletics scored those ten runs, but I told him that I lost $1,500." That was the difference in pay between players for the winning team and the losing team.

Blake's best season with the Cubs was 1928 when he won 17 games and led the league with four shutouts. He was released by the Cubs in 1931 and spent another seven seasons pitching in the minor leagues. He retired to his native West Virginia and worked as an electrician for a local power company.

Mike Gonzalez
Catcher, 1925-1929

Miguel Angel Gonzalez became the first Cuban manager in the major leagues after a career as a journeyman catcher.

He wasn't a great hitter, but Gonzalez had a rifle arm and defensive skills that would keep him in the major leagues for 17 years. Gonzalez spent time with five clubs, but became an everyday catcher only for the Cardinals. In 1925, St. Louis traded Gonzalez to the Cubs, where he spent five years as Gabby Hartnett's backup. He later turned to managing and spent 13 years as a coach with the Cardinals. In 1938 and 1940, he was named interim manager of the Redbirds. In his native Cuba, where he owned the Havana baseball club, Gonzalez was a beloved figure. He spent his later years as the island's chief talent scout.

William Wrigley and Joe McCarthy
Wrigley Field, 1926

When the Cubs finished in last place in 1925, owner William Wrigley decided to overhaul his team.

William Veeck urged Wrigley to take a chance on an unproven manager, Joe McCarthy, who'd been managing in Louisville the past six years. In the minors, McCarthy's teams won two championships and he proved a great judge of talent. In Chicago, McCarthy quickly stocked the Cubs with players he had seen in the minors. At his urging, the club signed three players who made an immediate impact: outfielders "Hack" Wilson and Riggs Stephenson, and pitcher Charlie Root.

By the time Wrigley secured stars Rogers Hornsby and Kiki Cuyler, the pieces were in place to make a run at a championship. In 1929, the Cubs won 98 games and finished in first place by 10 ½ games. Attendance more than doubled and Wrigley finally had his championship. The gamble paid off handsomely.

Guy Bush
Pitcher, 1923-1934

Guy Terrell Bush, a shy country boy from rural Mississippi, became one of the Cubs' most dependable pitchers.

Bush was signed by a scout who saw him throw two shutouts in a minor-league double-header for the Class D Greenville Swamp Angels in 1923. But young Bush was terrified of life in Chicago and so he left. He hid out in another minor league, pitching under an assumed name. Bush was tracked down and persuaded to catch a train for Chicago. The train was a Pullman, full of sleeping compartments. Unsure of what this meant, Bush decided to wait all night until a "day" train came along. Because of his unsophisticated ways, Bush's teammates thought him an easy mark. On the train trip to California for spring training in 1924, Bush was invited to join the rolling poker game. By the end of the trip, Bush had $400 of their money.

On the field, the Cubs brought Bush along slowly. He spent four years in relief before joining the starting rotation in 1927. In 1929, he won 18 games and in the World Series against the Philadelphia Athletics, was the only Cubs pitcher to win a game, thus avoiding a sweep.

When the Cubs won the pennant in 1932, Bush won 19 games. His resilient arm allowed him to be used out of the bullpen between starts and many of his victories came in relief. In 1933, he finally had a 20-win season. Despite winning 18 games the following year, Bush was traded to Pittsburgh prior to 1935.

In Pittsburgh, Bush allowed the final two home runs of Babe Ruth's career. In 1935, Ruth hit numbers 713 and 714 at Forbes Field and retired five days later.

Bush retired back to Mississippi to run the family farm. He died in 1985 at age 83.

Lewis "Hack" Wilson
Outfielder, 1926-1931

The only thing "Hack" Wilson hit longer and more frequently than a baseball was the bottle. In his prime, he was among the most feared sluggers in the major leagues. But a penchant for partying limited his career to seven productive years.

Lewis Robert Wilson had a hard life growing up in Pennsylvania. His parents never married, his mother died when he was seven and he dropped out of school to work in the steel mills. Pounding steel rivets with a sledgehammer forged Wilson's upper body into a mass of muscle. He had a size 18 neck, a massive chest and thick muscular calves, yet he wore a size 5 1/2 shoe. His ankles were so brittle that he had them wrapped prior to every game.

The New York Giants gave him his first shot at the majors in 1924, but sent him to Toledo after a slow start the next year. There he hit .343 and attracted the attention of Joe McCarthy, the manager in Louisville. When McCarthy was named manager of the Cubs, he convinced William Wrigley to purchase Wilson's contract for $5,000. It was a bargain.

Wilson arrived in Chicago for the 1926 season and soon became the Cubs' starting centerfielder. In four of the next five years, he led the National League in home runs. But Wilson proved more than just a slugger. In his first five years with the Cubs, Wilson never hit lower than .313. When the Cubs won the pennant in 1929, Wilson led the league with 159 RBI, while batting .345. Cubs fans were sure that not even Babe Ruth could have a better year. In 1930, Hack Wilson would prove them wrong.

Charlie Root
Pitcher, 1926-1941

With 201 wins, Charlie Root is the winningest pitcher in the history of the Cubs.

Root came to the Cubs after twice winning 20 games in the Pacific Coast League. He won 18 games his first year with Chicago and quickly became the workhorse of manager Joe McCarthy's staff. Root was efficient on the mound. He would regularly pitch a complete game in less than 90 minutes. In 1927, the best year of his career, he won 27 games and led the National League in wins and innings pitched.

But Root is best remembered for the defining moment of the 1932 World Series against the New York Yankees. It was Game 3 and the Cubs were playing at home at Wrigley Field, having lost the first two games. Emotions were hot and Commissioner Kennesaw Mountain Landis had to warn both teams about the foul language hurling from both dugouts. In the top of the fifth inning, with the game tied 4-4, Yankees slugger Babe Ruth came to the plate. In the first inning, Ruth had hit a three-run homer off Root. This time, Root quickly got two strikes on the Bambino. Ruth's next gesture is the subject of a debate that continues today. Did Babe Ruth, in raising his left hand, call his shot? Root said Ruth was simply indicating that he had one more strike left. Root's catcher, Gabby Hartnett, the closest player to Ruth, heard Ruth say, "It only takes one..." Either way, Hartnett called for an off-speed pitch that Root delivered on the outside part of the plate. Ruth sent the ball high into the centerfield stands, just to the right of the scoreboard. The Yankees won the game 7-5 and swept the series in four straight.

Root pitched in two more World Series, though unsuccessfully. Later in his career, he worked out of the bullpen and was an effective reliever. In 1941, at age 42, he won his 200th game. But at the end of the year, the Cubs released him.

In 1948, when Hollywood began filming *The Babe Ruth Story*, producers offered Root $5,000 to appear as himself in the film's crucial scene. Root turned it down. He also refused to allow his name to be used in the script.

Root spent six years as a major-league coach before retiring to run his cattle ranch in California. He died in 1970 at age 71.

Joe McCarthy
Manager, 1926-1930

Manager Joe McCarthy brought discipline and a winning tradition to the Cubs, building a foundation for the team's glory years.

McCarthy was a better manager than player. He first managed with Wilkes-Barre at the age of 26. While playing for Louisville, he was named manager and led that club to two American Association pennants. More importantly for the Cubs, who named him manager in 1926, McCarthy had a chance to scout the best talent in the minor leagues. When he moved to Chicago, McCarthy, 38, was able to quickly overhaul a team that had finished last the year before.

Midway through his first year, McCarthy established his authority when he released veteran pitcher Grover Cleveland Alexander. Generally, though, McCarthy was low-key. He was known for counseling players in private and never berating them in public. McCarthy tolerated off-field indiscretions so long as players came prepared to play hard.

When the Cubs won the 1929 NL pennant, but collapsed in the World Series, owner William Wrigley blamed McCarthy. The next year, when the Cubs finished second, Wrigley fired him.

McCarthy rebounded quickly. He was named manager of the New York Yankees in 1931. Over the next 15 seasons, he won seven World Series and built a dynasty with stars such as Lou Gehrig and Joe DiMaggio. In 1948, McCarthy spent two years managing the Boston Red Sox before resigning midway through the 1950 season.

In 24 seasons as a major-league manager, McCarthy never had a losing record. His .614 winning percentage is the highest in baseball history. In 1957, McCarthy was elected to the Hall of Fame. He died in 1978 at age 88.

Riggs Stephenson
Outfielder, 1926-1934

Jackson Riggs Stephenson was playing in Indianapolis in 1925 when Joe McCarthy, managing in Louisville, spotted him. The next year, when McCarthy was chosen to manage the Cubs, he nabbed Stephenson and made him the Cubs' left fielder.

Stephenson wasn't a power hitter. Only once did he hit more than eight home runs in a season. But his ability to hit doubles — a league-leading 46 in 1927 — drove up his batting average and earned him the nickname "Old Hoss" for carrying the team with his bat. In 1929, he batted .362 in a lineup stocked with stars. That year, Stephenson, Hack Wilson and Kiki Cuyler became the first outfield trio to each drive in more than 100 runs.

In 1934, the Cubs aquired slugger Chuck Klein and Stephenson was out. He spent the next four years playing and managing in the minors. In 1939, he returned to his home state of Alabama, where he operated a sawmill and lumberyard until his death in 1985.

Art Nehf
Pitcher, 1927-1929

At the height of his success, Art Nehf commanded the largest price ever paid for a ballplayer.

New York Giants manager John McGraw bought Nehf from the Boston Braves for $55,000 in 1919, a startling sum at the time. But the investment paid off. Nehf won 60 games over the next three years and came up big in the postseason. He won the deciding games of the 1921 and the 1922 World Series.

By the time he joined the Cubs, Nehf was 35 and his best years were behind him. He won 13 games in 1928 and another eight in 1929. But as a reliever in Game 4 of the 1929 World Series, Nehf failed to retire a batter as the Philadelphia Athletics scored 10 runs and blew the series wide open. He retired to Arizona and worked in the insurance business before slowed by a heart attack in 1932.

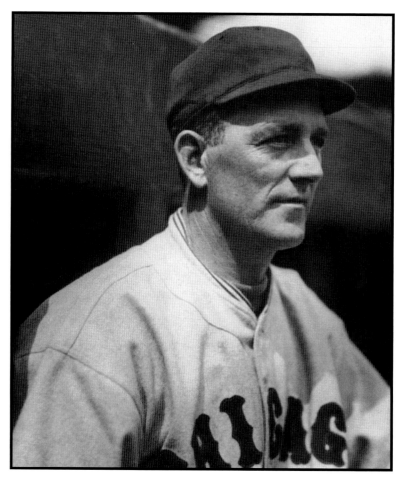

Hal Carlson
Pitcher, 1927-1930

Hal Carlson arrived in Chicago at the end of his career and near the end of his life.

Carlson debuted with Pittsburgh in 1917, but World War I intervened and Carlson signed up to serve in Europe. He became a machine gunner and saw plenty of action, including chemical warfare. After the war, when he returned to the Pirates, Carlson was used primarily as a reliever. He could no longer throw his trademark spitball because the league had outlawed it. But once he was traded to the Phillies in 1924, Carlson became a starter and won a career-high 17 games in 1926. He joined the Cubs in the middle of the 1927 season and won 12 games down the stretch.

One time, when Carlson complained of a sore arm, the Cubs' trainer rubbed his arm with Coca-Cola, saying it was a secret home remedy. Carlson threw a complete game victory that day, and thereafter, insisted on the secret treatment before every game. In the spring of 1930, Carlson discovered more serious health problems. X-rays showed his lungs were severely damaged by the poison gasses he inhaled during the war. On May 28, 1930, surrounded by his Cubs teammates, he died of a stomach hemorrhage in his hotel room. Carlson was 38.

Charlie Grimm
First baseman, 1925-1936

Long before Ernie Banks, Charlie Grimm was the original "Mr. Cub." He spent more than six decades in professional baseball, managed the Cubs on three separate occasions and took the team to three World Series.

Grimm's easy-going manner and penchant for pranks earned him the nickname "Jolly Cholly" when he first played in Pittsburgh. Grimm loved beer, German food and playing to an audience. But the Pirates tired of his antics and after the 1924 season, traded him to the Cubs. The first baseman was a steady, if average hitter whose real value lay in his on-field leadership and ability to keep teammates loose. In the clubhouse, he played the banjo along with his pranks.

In the middle of the 1932 season, Grimm replaced Rogers Hornsby as Cubs manager and led the team to the National League pennant. A second pennant followed in 1935. Midway through 1938, Grimm turned the club over to Gabby Hartnett and moved to the radio booth as a broadcaster. But he missed being on the field and so, two years later, Grimm moved to Milwaukee as manager. There, he won the minor league World Series in 1943. The next year, the Cubs brought him back as manager. And in 1945, under his leadership, the Cubs went to the World Series. It would turn out to be the Cubs' last series appearance of the 20th Century.

Grimm later held a variety of positions in the Cubs organization, including one final turn as manager in 1960. He was a sought-after speaker on the Chicago banquet circuit, telling stories and playing his banjo. When the Wrigley family finally sold the team in 1981, Grimm's tenure with the team came to an end. He retired to Arizona where he died in 1983. A loyal Cub to the end, Grimm's ashes were scattered over Wrigley Field.

Elwood "Woody" English
Infielder, 1927-1936

Woody English, 20, was one of several young players that manager Joe McCarthy recruited to rebuild the Cubs.

As lead-off hitter, English's job was to get on base ahead of the team's sluggers. English played shortstop and when Rogers Hornsby arrived to play second in 1929, the Cubs had one of the league's best double-play combinations. The duo roomed together on the road, and with Hornsby's tips on hitting, English had his best year in 1930, batting .335 and hitting 14 homers. In 1932, the Cubs moved him to third base to make room for Billy Jurges at shortstop.

English was a member of the first National League All-Star team in 1933. But by 1935, he became a part-time player and in 1937, he was traded to Brooklyn. English retired two years later to Chicago's north side, where he operated a saloon for five years. Later, he managed the Grand Rapids Chicks in the All-American Womens' Baseball League.

Pat Malone
Pitcher, 1928-1934

Perce Leigh Malone was a hell-raising right-hander with an overpowering fastball and a defiance for authority.

Growing up in Altoona, Pennsylvania, Malone was the leader of a street gang. At 15, he took a job shoveling coal on the passing trains and developed massive arm and shoulder muscles. He also developed a short temper and a fondness for the drink, a combination that kept him in the minor leagues for seven years. But after he twice won 20 games, the Cubs purchased him for $25,000 in 1928. Malone lost his first seven games, but manager Joe McCarthy believed in him and kept him in the starting rotation. By the end of the season, Malone had won 18 games. The next year, he led the National League in wins, strikeouts and shutouts. And in 1930, he was one of only two pitchers in the league to win 20 games.

Malone's success came in spite of his late-night sprees. He and Hack Wilson were inseparable drinking buddies and, during Prohibition, their status as ballplayers gave them the run of Chicago's speakeasys. The Cubs management became so concerned about Malone's carousing that they paid for his wife to travel with the team. It had little effect.

In 1931, Rogers Hornsby became the Cubs manager. Hornsby didn't drink or smoke and he didn't like players who did, players like Malone. The two feuded and Malone's wins tapered off. Malone also continued to get in trouble off the field. In 1931, encouraged by his buddy Hack Wilson, Malone beat up two Chicago sportswriters while the team was waiting to board a train for a road trip. Malone's adventures continued until 1934, when manager Charlie Grimm had seen enough. Grimm benched Malone for the last six weeks of the season and then traded him to the Cardinals.

In St. Louis, Malone again fought with his manager and was traded to the Yankees before he ever threw a pitch. Reunited with McCarthy in New York, Malone was converted to a reliever and in 1936, he led the American League in saves and relief wins. At age 36, he spent one final year in the minors before returning to Altoona to operate a cafe.

In 1943, Pat Malone visited his old teammate, Hack Wilson, in Baltimore. The two spent two days out on the town, drinking. After Malone took the train back to Altoona, he had to walk home through a driving rainstorm. Ten days later, he died of pneumonia at age 40.

Rogers Hornsby
Second baseman, 1929-1932

Rogers Hornsby was the greatest right-handed hitter in major league history, but once he left St. Louis, his abrasive personality kept him on the move.

After 11 seasons and six batting titles with the Cardinals, Hornsby was traded when he wouldn't agree to a contract. He played one season with the New York Giants, then a season with the Boston Braves. In 1929, Cubs owner William Wrigley sent $200,000 and five players to Boston for Hornsby. It was a staggering sum of money, even for a player with Hornsby's credentials. But by season's end, the "Rajah," as he was known, proved to be worth every cent. Hornsby's bat made the Cubs' already potent line-up almost unstoppable. He was named the league's MVP, batting .380, with 39 home runs and 149 RBI. The Cubs won the 1929 National League pennant by 10½ games.

In 1931, Hornsby replaced Joe McCarthy as Cubs manager, but the team played poorly and his constant ridicule wore thin with players. The following year, Hornsby's gambling at the racetrack became the subject of an investigation by Commissioner Landis. On August 2, 1932, with the team struggling to stay in the race, the Cubs replaced Hornsby with first baseman Charlie Grimm.

Hornsby became a baseball gypsy, moving from job to job to stay close to the game he loved. In 1932, he managed the lowly St. Louis Browns for four-plus years and later spent several seasons managing in the minors. Hornsby returned to the majors as manager of the Browns and the Reds in the 1950's, but as always, his brusque manner poisoned his relationship with players. He held a variety of positions in the minor leagues before returning to the Cubs in 1958 as a coach for two years. He was elected to the Hall of Fame in 1942 and died in 1963.

Hazen "Kiki" Cuyler
Outfielder, 1928-1935

"Kiki" Cuyler was a speedy outfielder with a rifle arm who helped spur the Cubs to a pennant.

Adding Cuyler to an outfield with Hack Wilson and Riggs Stephenson gave the Cubs the league's most-lethal outfield. Cuyler ran wild and led the league in stolen bases for three consecutive years. In 1929 and 1930, he hit .360 and .355 respectively.

Cuyler was never more valuable than during the final months of the 1932 season. His clutch hitting spurred the Cubs to the pennant. Cuyler hit .365 the final month of the season, helping the Cubs streak past the Pirates.

The next year, Cuyler missed half of the season with injuries, but he rebounded in 1934 to bat .338. When the Cubs started slowly in 1935, they let Cuyler go. He signed with the Cincinnati Reds for two years, then spent one final season in Brooklyn.

Cuyler spent six-plus seasons managing in the Southern Association and also coached briefly with the Cubs during World War II. He was a coach with the Red Sox when he died suddenly of a heart attack in 1950 at age 50. In 1968, Cuyler was elected to the Hall of Fame.

Rogers Hornsby, Hack Wilson, Al Simmons, Jimmie Foxx
World Series, 1929

Four future Hall of Famers posed for photographers before Game 1 of the 1929 World Series at Philadelphia's Shibe Park.

The Athletics won the Series in five games. Their line-up of sluggers hit six home runs and scored 26 runs. Their pitching staff struck out 50 Cubs batters and limited them to one home run. Hack Wilson was the Cubs' lone bright spot, hitting .471 for the series. Hornsby struggled, batting .238. Simmons and Foxx each had two home runs.

Lon Warneke
Pitcher, 1930-1936; 1942-1943; 1945

Three times during the 1930's, Lon Warneke won 20 games for the Cubs.

A tall stringbean with a blazing fastball, Warneke was a country boy from rural Arkansas. His first season with the Cubs, manager Rogers Hornsby used him primarily in relief. But once a flaw in his delivery was corrected, Warneke became a starter and a winner. In 1932, Warneke led the National League with 22 wins. In 1933, he led the league in complete games and was named to pitch in the first All-Star game. Warneke won 20 games each of the next two years. He opened the 1934 season with back-to-back one-hitters, and in the 1935 World Series against the Detroit Tigers, he earned the team's only two victories.

Warneke won another 16 games in 1936, but the Cubs traded him to the St. Louis Cardinals after the season. It was a bad deal for the Cubs. Warneke was a consistent winner in his five years in St. Louis. There, he was nicknamed the "Arkansas Hummingbird" by a local sportswriter and joined the remnants of the famed "Gas House Gang." In 1939, Warneke one-hit the Cubs and in 1941, he threw a no-hitter against the world champion Cincinnati Reds. The Cubs wanted him back so badly that they gave St. Louis $75,000 for him in the middle of the 1942 season. But at age 33, Warneke's arm was gone. He won only 10 games for the Cubs over three seasons. He retired after the 1945 season.

Warneke's desire to stay around baseball led him to become an umpire. After three years learning the craft in the Pacific Coast League, he spent seven years back in the National League calling balls and strikes. In 1956, Warneke left baseball to return to Arkansas. In 1962, he was elected a civil court judge in Garland County. Warneke died in 1976 at age 67.

Hack Wilson's eyes
1930

In 1930, Lewis "Hack" Wilson had one of the greatest years in major league history. He hit 56 home runs and drove in 191 runs, leading the major leagues in both categories. In the next 70 years, only Cleveland's Manny Ramirez would come close to challenging Wilson's RBI record with 165 in 1999.

When you remember that players of Wilson's era played a 154-game schedule compared to today's 162-game season, the feat means even more.

Now consider this: that same year, Wilson led the league in walks and strike-outs.

Wilson's season was highlighted by producing 54 runs in the month of August. It remains the all-time record for RBI in a single month. The sportswriters named Wilson the league's most valuable player of 1930.

Bobby and Hack Wilson
Chicago, 1930

1930 was Hack Wilson's best year and he was mobbed everywhere he went. Hundreds of fans waited outside ballparks across the country, hoping for a look at baseball's newest star. In Chicago, Wilson needed police escorts to leave Wrigley Field after a home game. But he enjoyed his celebrity. He fielded dozens of endorsement offers and even spent one off-season on the vaudeville circuit with a song-and-dance routine. But the liquor and late nights began to take their toll. After Wilson hit just 13 home runs in 1931 and continued feuding with manager Rogers Hornsby, the Cubs traded him to Brooklyn in 1932. Wilson tried to turn his career around, but it was too late. By 1935, he was out of the majors.

Wilson returned to Martinsburg, West Virginia, and worked a variety of jobs. His home life was anything but tranquil and in 1937, his wife Virginia filed for divorce and was given custody of their son, Bobby. Hack married a waitress and began wandering the country, looking for ways to make a buck. In 1948, when he was working at the city parks department in Baltimore, Wilson died broke and alone at age 48.

The mortuary notified Bobby, 22, of his father's death. The son wired back: "Am not responsible." Wilson's body lay unclaimed for three days until baseball officials paid to ship the body back to Martinsburg for burial. The local Elk's Lodge passed the hat and raised the $3,000 needed to cover funeral expenses. Bobby didn't attend. After college, Bobby became a school teacher and later, a principal. He never married and died himself in 1985 at age 60.

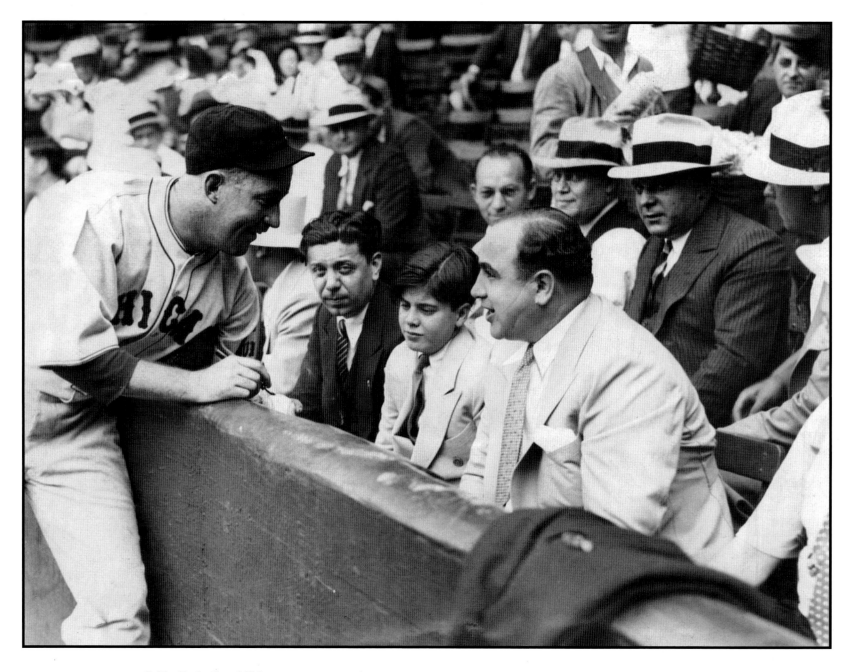

Gabby Hartnett and Al Capone
Wrigley Field, 1931

Chicago's most notorious citizen took in the first game of the annual City Series between the Cubs and White Sox on September 30, 1931.

Accompanied by his son, Al, Jr., and several bodyguards, Al Capone chatted casually with Cubs catcher Gabby Hartnett before the game. Capone had asked Hartnett to sign a baseball for his nephew. A local photographer recorded the moment and the photo ran in the newspaper the following day. When Commissioner Kennesaw Mountain Landis saw the photo, he insisted that a warning be posted in every major league clubhouse that said: "No fraternizing between fans and players." Less than 30 days later, Capone was convicted of tax evasion. He spent the next eight years in federal prisons in Atlanta and Alcatraz before dying in Miami in 1947.

Guy Bush
Chicago, 1931

During the Depression, ballplayers had to make ends meet like everyone else. Cubs pitcher Guy Bush spent his off-seasons operating a gas station near Wrigley Field. After seven years with the Cubs, the "Mississippi Mudcat," who once feared big-city life, had invested his baseball earnings wisely. Bush developed a reputation as a real city-slicker, known for his dapper dress and cruising around Chicago in his sports car.

Rogers Hornsby and Charlie Grimm
Wrigley Field, 1931

Grumbling continued after the Cubs finished third in 1931 under manager Rogers Hornsby. The players resented Hornsby's cold demeanor and insulting comments. The straight-laced Hornsby had only one vice: gambling. He loved to play the ponies, but he wasn't very lucky. When it became known in 1932 that Hornsby had borrowed more than $11,000 from Cubs players to cover his losses, team president William Veeck fired him.

Charlie Grimm took over the club on August 3. The players, happy to be rid of the heavy-handed Hornsby, responded to Grimm's easy-going style. The team went 37-20 down the stretch and won the 1932 National League pennant.

Kiki Cuyler, Gabby Hartnett, Riggs Stephenson, Charlie Grimm
Polo Grounds, 1932

With the season nearly over and the National League pennant in sight, four of the Cubs' biggest bats took time to pose for photographers. Except for Riggs Stephenson, the group didn't put up the awesome numbers of the 1929 team, but they won when it counted and their timely hitting in clutch situations made the difference. They won the pennant.

In the World Series against the Yankees, they were simply overmatched. The Yankees outscored the Cubs, 37-19, and swept the Series in four games.

Stan Hack and Evar Swanson
Spring Training, 1933

Stan Hack was considered the fastest man on the Cubs when he joined in 1932. His speed was put to the test the following spring.

Chicago White Sox outfielder Evar Swanson held the record for the fastest time around the bases, at 13.3 seconds. Hollywood film comedian Joe E. Brown put up $500 and a trophy if Hack and Swanson would race each other in spring training. They did, and the 30-year-old Swanson beat the 23-year old Hack.

Swanson's time around the bases is a record that stands today.

**Philip K. Wrigley and Charlie Grimm
Spring Training, 1934**

When William Wrigley died in 1932, his son Philip assumed ownership of the Cubs. For the next 20 years, Wrigley kept the team's spring training camp at Catalina Island, off the California coast. The family's island estate featured a zoo with some exotic animals, and some not so extraordinary. Cubs manager Charlie Grimm, always one for a practical joke, didn't need much coaching from photographers to pose with his boss and a goat. Under the son's leadership, the Cubs' on-field performance wouldn't prove so funny.

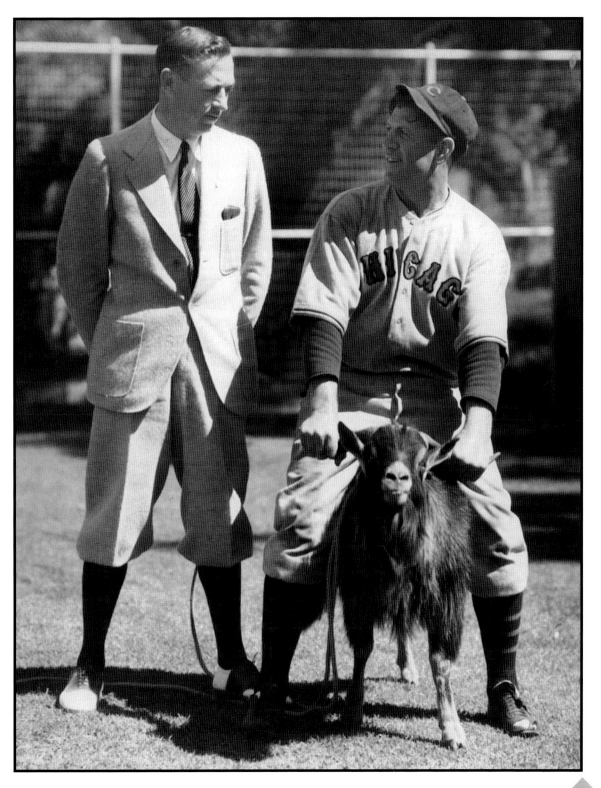

"Babe" Herman
Outfielder, 1933-1934

Floyd Caves Herman was never a graceful outfielder, but his skill with the bat made him one of the National League's most feared hitters — until he got to Chicago.

Herman was one of the league's best sluggers during his six years with the Brooklyn Dodgers. Three times, he hit above .340. In 1930, he hit a club record .393 with 35 home runs. In 1932, after he was traded to the Reds, he batted .326 and led the league in triples.

With numbers like these, Cubs fans were ecstatic when the team announced that Herman would be coming to Chicago for the 1933 season. But Herman batted .289 his first year, and even though he led the team in home runs and RBI, he was booed by the Wrigley Field faithful. Herman also was maligned in the press for mishandling fly balls. Stories were written that he had balls bouncing off his head. It was all an exaggeration, but the reputation followed Herman throughout his career. After a second season with the Cubs, when he hit .304 and was second on the team in RBI, Herman was traded to Pittsburgh.

He would play for three different teams over the next three years before spending six years in the Pacific Coast League. In retirement, Herman operated a turkey farm in California.

Frank Demaree
Outfielder, 1932-1933; 1935-1938

Frank Demaree was an All-Star hitter who played in the shadow of the Cubs' biggest stars. In 1933, Demaree filled in when Cubs centerfielder Kiki Cuyler broke his leg in spring training. The next year, back in the minors, Demaree had a monster year, hitting .383 with 45 home runs. *The Sporting News* named him the Pacific Coast League's most valuable player. In 1935, Demaree replaced Cuyler as the Cubs' centerfielder and batted .325. In 1937, he batted .324 and his 115 RBI were the second highest in the National League

Demaree was chosen to be the starting centerfielder of the 1936 and 1937 All-Star Games. Traded to the New York Giants after the 1938 season, Demaree played another six years in the majors, mostly as a back-up. Demaree retired to California, where he worked for a movie studio in Los Angeles. He died in 1958 at age 48.

"Tuck" Stainbeck
Outfielder, 1934-1937

George Tucker Stainbeck spent 13 years in the majors, but only two as an everyday player. His best season was his first. In 1934, he hit .306 as the Cubs' fourth outfielder. His ability to run down fly balls kept him in the majors. His weak hitting kept him from playing every day. In 1938, Stainbeck was traded, along with two other players and $185,000, to the Cardinals for pitcher Dizzy Dean. His only other season as a regular came with the Brooklyn Dodgers in 1939. When he left baseball, Stainbeck returned to California and later worked in the Los Angeles Dodgers' ticket office for 20 years.

Dolf Camilli
First baseman, 1933-1934

First baseman Dolf Camilli hit 239 major-league home runs. Unfortunately for Cubs fans, he hit only six with Chicago. In one of the worst trades in Cubs history, the team sent Camilli packing after his rookie year.

Camilli came to the Cubs after four strong seasons in the Pacific Coast League. Prone to strike-outs, he played mostly off the bench and appeared in only 46 games. The next spring, the Cubs sent Camilli and $30,000 to the Phillies for aging first baseman Don Hurst. Hurst wound up playing only 51 games for the Cubs. Camilli, with his huge hands and quick reflexes, became one of the league's premier defensive first basemen. He also was a superb run producer. He hit 20-plus homers each of the next eight years and had five years with more than 100 RBI. In 1941, Camilli led the National League in home runs and RBI and was named its most valuable player. In 1945, he retired at age 38.

In 1946, Camilli began coaching in the minors. Starting in 1951, he spent 20 years as a major league scout.

Chuck Klein
Outfielder, 1934-1936

Desperate to replace the departed Hack Wilson's power numbers, the Cubs sent $65,000 and three players to the Phillies in 1933 for Chuck Klein, a one-man record-wrecking crew.

In six years with Philadelphia, Klein had led the National League in hits and RBI twice, home runs four times and stolen bases once. He was the league's most valuable player in 1932. And in 1933, he had a triple-crown year, hitting .368, with 28 home runs and 120 RBI. Klein could do it all.

Unfortunately someone forgot to remind the Cubs that the left-handed Klein played half his games in Philadelphia's tiny Baker Bowl, whose right-field wall was only 280 feet from home plate. As a dead-pull hitter, Klein's short home runs in Philadelphia turned into long outs at Wrigley Field. Klein admitted publicly that the pressure of playing for a contending team like the Cubs bothered him. With the lowly Phillies, he said, "Nobody cared if I hit or didn't hit. Here, they watch you on every pitch." Chuck Klein hit 20 and 21 home runs in his two years with the Cubs.

Early in the 1936 season, a frustrated front office shipped Klein back to the Phillies, along with a check for $50,000. The Cubs had now spent $115,000 on a player who was gone after only two seasons. It was to become a pattern that would haunt the franchise for the next 30 years.

Klein spent eight more years in the majors before retiring after the 1944 season. He operated a tavern in Philadelphia for several years, but developed a drinking problem. Later, in Indianapolis, he suffered a stroke. Klein died broke in 1958 at age 53. He was elected to the Hall of Fame in 1980.

Billy Jurges
Shortstop, 1931-1938; 1946-1947

Billy Jurges was a smooth-fielding shortstop who teamed with second baseman Billy Herman to give the Cubs their best double-play combination since the days of Joe Tinker and Johnny Evers.

Jurges was a scrappy player from the Bronx whose career kept getting interrupted. In 1932, a young showgirl in love with him entered his Chicago hotel room and shot him twice as he tried to wrestle the gun away. Jurges survived, but missed about a month of the season recovering from his wounds. Early in 1934, Jurges collapsed in the clubhouse before a game and was rushed to the hospital for an emergency appendectomy. In Game 3 of the 1935 World Series, Jurges was fined for using "vile and unprintable" language toward umpire George Moriarity.

In the middle of the 1938 season, Jurges was summoned to Philip Wrigley's office and offered the job of Cubs manager. Charlie Grimm was out. Jurges declined the offer and said veteran catcher Gabby Hartnett was more deserving. Wrigley gave the job to Hartnett and the Cubs went on to win the 1938 National League pennant. At the end of the season, the Cubs traded Jurges to the New York Giants. So much for doing the right thing.

In New York, Jurges spent seven years anchoring the Giants infield, where his fiery demeanor was again on display. In 1939, Jurges spit on umpire George Magerkurth twice during a heated war of words that escalated to blows. Only the umpire's admission that he threw the first punch limited Jurges' suspension to 10 days. In 1946, Jurges returned to the Cubs for parts of two seasons, then retired. He spent time managing in the minors before spending one year as manager of the Boston Red Sox in 1959. Jurges later spent 20 years as a scout for the Cubs.

Clay Bryant
Pitcher, 1935-1940

Clay Bryant spent six years in the majors, all of them with the Cubs.

Bryant started as a reliever, but in 1938, the big right-hander with an overpowering fastball was added to the Cubs' starting rotation. He won 19 games, but had the dubious distinction of leading the National League in walks and strike-outs. Bryant was an unusually good hitter for a pitcher. His career batting average was .266 and in 1937, he hit a grand slam in the 10th inning of a game at Boston.

Suffering arm problems, Bryant retired after the 1940 season and began his second career in baseball, managing in the minor leagues for more than 20 years. His Dodger farm teams won three titles. Later, he also served two stints as pitching coach with the Cleveland Indians.

Billy Herman
Second baseman, 1931-1941

Billy Herman was the greatest second baseman of his era. He was named to the All-Star team 10 times and batted .304 over his career.

At 22, Herman took over second base from Rogers Hornsby and hit .314 in his first full season. Herman was teamed with shortstop Billy Jurges and the two formed a dazzling defensive combination. Herman had excellent range, able to play some hitters behind second base and others on the outfield grass. The result was that Herman led the National League in putouts seven times. Batting second in the Cubs line-up, Herman was equally effective at the plate. He was known for his skill at executing the hit-and-run play. Hall of Fame manager Leo Durocher called Herman "an absolute master at hitting behind the runner." In 1935, Herman hit .341 and led the league in hits and doubles. In 1939 he led the league with 18 triples.

In 1941, the Cubs got a new manager, Jimmie Wilson, who considered the veteran Herman a threat to his job. Eleven games into the season, the Cubs traded Herman to Brooklyn. The Dodgers won the National League pennant that year. The Cubs finished sixth.

Herman spent two years in the Navy during World War II and when he returned in 1946, he was 36 and near the end of the line. After brief stays with the Braves and Pittsburgh, he retired in 1947 to become manager of the Pirates. He lasted just one season. Herman spent the next 30 years as a minor league manager, scout and major league coach. In 1965, he was named manager of the Boston Red Sox, but was fired late the following season.

Herman was elected to the Hall of Fame in 1975. He died in 1992 at age 83.

Phil Cavarretta
First baseman, 1934-1953

Phil Cavarretta was a Chicago high school star who joined the Cubs at 18 and stayed for 20 years.

Cavarretta had a tryout at Wrigley Field in 1933 and won a ticket to the minors. A year later, he got a late-season call-up from the Cubs. In his first game as a starter, the rookie homered and scored the game's only run.

Cubs manager Charlie Grimm made Cavarretta his special project that year, tutoring him on the finer points of playing first base. The next spring, the 18-year-old became the Cubs' everyday first baseman. That fall, he played in the World Series against the Detroit Tigers.

Augie Galan
Outfielder, 1934-1941

Augie Galan had only one good arm, yet he spent seven seasons playing in the Cubs' outfield.

As a child, Galan fell out of a tree and shattered his right elbow. He was afraid to tell his parents and when the arm finally healed, he could bend it only half way. Undaunted, Galan left home at 19 and joined the San Francisco Seals, where he played alongside a young Joe DiMaggio.

The Cubs signed Galan after he batted .356 in 1933. The next year in Chicago, he batted .314 and led the league in stolen bases and runs scored.

Galan's career contained a couple of notable firsts. In 1936, he became the first Cub to hit a home run in an All-Star game. And in 1937, he became the first National League player to hit a home run from both sides of the plate in the same game.

But knee injuries plagued Galan. In 1940, he broke his knee cap when he ran into the outfield wall in Philadelphia. He missed the second half of the season and later struggled to play with a steel knee brace. By the middle of 1941, he was hitting only .208 and the Cubs released him. Galan joined the Brooklyn Dodgers and, starting in 1944, he batted over .300 for the next four seasons.

Galan retired after the 1949 season at age 37. In 1953, he managed the Oakland Oaks in the Pacific Coast League for one year. He died in 1993.

Larry French
Pitcher, 1935-1941

Only World War II could keep Larry French from winning 200 games in the major leagues.

French never tired of taking the mound. During the 1930's, only Giants pitcher Carl Hubbell threw more innings than French. When the big left-hander joined the Cubs in 1935 after six years with the Pirates, he quickly became the workhorse of the rotation. French frequently flirted with no-hitters and had several bids spoiled in the late innings. A screwball pitcher, French threw 40 shutouts in his career, 21 of them with the Cubs. But when he hurt his pitching hand and won only five games in 1941, the Cubs traded him to Brooklyn. There, French taught himself to throw a knuckleball and in 1942, he rebounded to go 15-4 with a 1.83 ERA for the Dodgers.

When the 1942 season ended, French was three victories shy of 200 wins. He also had a wife and a small child. Nevertheless, he enlisted as an officer in the Navy and was sent to Europe, where he commanded a landing craft in the days following the invasion of Normandy. Later, he served on a battleship in the Pacific. In 1946, French returned from the war at age 38, but he never had a chance to pitch in the majors again.

As a civilian, French operated a car dealership and sold insurance, then spent another 18 years in the Navy.

Bill Lee
Pitcher, 1934-1943; 1947

Bill Lee became the Cubs' pitching ace when he was purchased from the Cardinals in 1934. In his first two starts, Lee threw consecutive shutouts. The next year, he won 20 games. Through most of his career in Chicago, Lee was an overpowering pitcher.

But the big right-hander with the high leg-kick was at his best during the 1938 championship season. He won 22 games and had the highest winning percentage in the National League. In addition, Lee's 2.66 ERA and nine shutouts were also tops in the league. During one stretch of games in September, he threw 39 consecutive scoreless innings. He pitched in all three games of the series against the Pirates that decided the 1938 National League pennant. He saved two leads and won the final game.

For all his size and success on the mound, Lee kept to himself at the ballpark. Everyone knew his rules. Lee took exactly four warm-up pitches before each inning, he never allowed himself to be photographed on the day he pitched and he never allowed anyone to touch his glove.

In 1940, Lee's eyesight began to go bad. He couldn't see the catcher's signals and as a result, he won fewer games. He tried wearing glasses on the mound, but his effectiveness was gone. The Cubs traded Lee in August 1943. He won another 30 games for the Phillies and Braves before returning briefly to the Cubs in 1947. He retired to his Louisiana farm the next year, where he eventually lost his sight. Lee died in 1977 at age 67.

Larry French, Lon Warneke, Bill Lee, Charlie Root
1935 starting pitchers

The Cubs "big four" pitching staff had a superb year in 1935, despite the World Series.

Lon Warneke and Bill Lee both won 20 games. Larry French and Charlie Root combined to win 32. And together, Cubs pitchers led the National League with 81 complete games and a 3.26 ERA.

In the World Series against Detroit, Warneke won Games 1 and 5 and limited the Tigers to a single run. Unfortunately, those were the only two wins for the Cubs. Detroit took the Series in six games.

Ken O'Dea
Catcher, 1935-1938

James Kenneth O'Dea spent his 12-year career in the major leagues as a backup catcher. He occasionally started for the Cubs whenever Gabby Hartnett needed a day off or was injured. On one such occasion in mid-1936, O'Dea went on a hitting streak. The Cubs won 15 straight games and O'Dea's bat carried the team, going 18 for 37. Still, his brief success could not eclipse the proven talent of a future Hall of Famer like Hartnett, and so O'Dea returned to the bench.

After the 1938 season, the Cubs traded O'Dea to the New York Giants, where he spent the next three years backing up catcher Harry Danning. In 1942, O'Dea was traded to the St. Louis Cardinals, where he appeared as a pinch-hitter in three straight World Series.

James "Tex" Carleton
Pitcher, 1935-1938

Tex Carleton won exactly 100 games in the majors and was a consistent winner for the Cardinals, then the Cubs.

After winning 20 games for the Houston Buffaloes in 1931, St. Louis brought him to the big leagues along with teammate Dizzy Dean. Carleton won 43 games in three years, but the Cardinals traded him to the Cubs after the 1934 season. The tall Texan's best season for Chicago was 1937, when he posted a 16-8 record and led Cubs pitchers with a 3.15 ERA. When Carleton developed arm problems, the Cubs sent him to the minors in 1939. He was signed by the Brooklyn Dodgers and in 1940, threw a no-hitter against the Cincinnati Reds. After another year back in the minors, he retired following the 1941 season.

Cubs World Series train
Chicago, 1935

Team mascot Paul Dominic (in uniform) is surrounded by members of the Cubs as they head to the 1935 World Series in Detroit after having won their third National League pennant in seven years. The Cubs had last met the Tigers in the 1908 World Series, which the Cubs won in five games. This time, the teams would split the first two games in Detroit. They played Games 3, 4 and 5 in Chicago and the Tigers left town holding a 3-2 lead. In Game 6, back in Detroit, with the game tied 3-3 in the top of the ninth, Cubs third baseman Stan Hack led off with a triple. But his teammates left him stranded and the Tigers scored in the bottom of the inning. Detroit took the game and the Series.

Joe Tinker and Johnny Evers
Wrigley Field, 1937

When Joe Tinker and Johnny Evers were reunited in Chicago in 1937, the two hadn't seen each other in 14 years. Their bitter feud had mellowed and when they met in a Chicago hotel, after a moment's hesitation, they threw their arms around each other and cried.

Later that summer, they returned to Wrigley Field for an old-timers' day game and dedicated a plaque to the memory of their departed teammate and leader, Frank Chance. That night, the two men attended a boxing match and saw Joe Louis win the heavyweight championship for the first time.

Charles "Gabby" Hartnett
Spring training, 1937

Gabby Hartnett hit the most famous home run in Chicago Cubs history.

It happened late in 1938 when the Cubs were chasing the Pittsburgh Pirates for the National League crown. The Pirates had started the final month of the season with a seven-game lead. But the streaking Cubs caught fire and with five days remaining in the season, the Pirates came to Wrigley Field with only a 1½-game lead. In the first game of the series, Cubs pitchers Dizzy Dean and Bill Lee held Pittsburgh to a single run and the Cubs won, 2-1. The next day, with the teams tied 5-5, darkness set in after eight innings. The umpires agreed to play the ninth inning in hopes of deciding the crucial game. The Pirates batters were retired in order. The first two Cubs batters also failed to reach base. All hopes rested on the shoulders of Hartnett, the team's veteran catcher and manager.

Hartnett swung and missed the first pitch from Pirates' pitcher Mace Brown. He fouled off the next pitch and was in the hole, 0-2. Hartnett connected on Brown's next delivery and sent the ball over the wall into the left-field stands. Darkness made the crowd unsure of where the ball had landed. Only when the umpire signaled that it was indeed a home run did the crowd of more than 34,000 race onto the field.

Hartnett was mobbed as he rounded the bases. He had to fight his way through the crowd to reach home plate and officially make the Cubs 6-5 winners. Hartnett's hit became known as the "Homer in the Gloamin" and gave the Cubs a half-game lead over the Pirates.

Chicago trounced Pittsburgh the next day, 10-1, essentially ending the pennant race. Two days later, the Cubs clinched the pennant in St. Louis.

Stan Hack
Third baseman, 1932-1947
Manager, 1954-1956

Stan Hack spent his entire 16-year career with the Chicago Cubs and became one of the franchise's most popular players.

Nicknamed "Smiling Stan" for his easy-going manner, Hack became a fixture at third base. He was a smooth fielder who gathered ground balls with ease. He led all NL third basemen in putouts for four straight years, starting in 1938.

Offensively, Hack was a career .301 hitter who twice led the National League in hits. He never hit for much power, but as the team's lead-off hitter, his job was to get on base in front of the sluggers. As a result, beginning in 1936, Hack scored at least 100 runs for six straight years. Always a threat on the basepaths, he was a four-time All-Star who twice led the league in stolen bases.

In the 1935 World Series against Detroit, with the score tied 5-5 in Game 6, Hack hit a triple to lead off the ninth inning, but he was left stranded. The Tigers scored a run in the bottom of the inning to win the series. Later, when Hack returned to Tiger Stadium for the 1941 All-Star Game, his first act was to go out on the field and take a look at third base. When asked by sportswriters what he was doing, Hack replied, "I wanted to see if I was still standing out there waiting for someone to drive me home."

After the 1943 season, Hack retired rather than continue playing for Cubs manager Jimmie Wilson. When Wilson was fired early the next season, manager Charlie Grimm convinced Hack to return. The following year, his last season as an everyday player, Hack hit .323 and helped lead the Cubs to the 1945 pennant. He retired for good after the 1947 season with 2,193 hits. Hack spent six years managing in the minors before being named to replace Phil Cavarretta as the Cubs manager in 1954. In three seasons under Hack, the Cubs managed no better than a sixth-place showing.

Later in life, Hack operated a restaurant in Grand Detour, Illinois. He died in 1979 at age 70.

Charlie Grimm and Philip K. Wrigley
Spring Training, 1938

Cubs manager Charlie Grimm was only too happy to show team owner Philip Wrigley a new banner commemorating the Cubs legacy. Grimm is pointing out the stars representing the team's World Series victories in 1907 and 1908. The other 14 stars represent the team's National League pennants, dating back to 1876.

At the time this photo was taken, the Cubs had been to three World Series in nine years. The Cubs won two more pennants in 1938 and 1945, but Cubs fans have waited more than half a century for another.

"Dizzy" Dean
Pitcher, 1938-1941

During the height of the Depression, the National League's greatest gate attraction was St. Louis Cardinals pitcher "Dizzy" Dean.

Dean arrived in the majors with a blazing fastball and a reputation for self-promotion. He led the league in strikeouts for four straight years, starting in 1932. In 1933, he won 20 games. The next year, he won 30. There hasn't been another 30-game winner in the National League since.

Along with teammate "Pepper" Martin, Dean was the leader of the Cardinals' famous "Gashouse Gang." In six seasons with the Cardinals, he won 133 games. But a batted ball broke his toe in the 1937 All-Star Game and Dean aggravated the injury by pitching again 10 days later. Dean had to change his pitching motion to compensate, but the new delivery put too much strain on his shoulder and his arm went bad.

After the 1937 season, Cubs management decided to take a chance on "Ol' Diz" despite his sore arm. His arrival boosted attendance, but fans soon found his fastball had been replaced with a "nothing ball," as Dean called it. He was forced to get by on guts and out-thinking opposing hitters. In 1938, Dean won seven games for the Cubs and helped the team return to the World Series. But at age 27, he was washed up. He continued to pitch for another three seasons, but won only nine more games in the majors. Dean retired in 1941.

With his colorful expressions and outlandish grammar, Dean gained a new audience as a broadcaster in St. Louis. In 1953, he was elected to the Hall of Fame. Dean died in 1974.

Bill "Swish" Nicholson
Outfielder, 1939-1948

Bill Nicholson's nickname came from the powerful practice swings he took before every at-bat. Fans in Brooklyn yelled "swish!" and the name stuck.

Nicholson was a top home-run hitter during World War II. For five straight years, he hit more than 20 home runs. In 1943 and 1944, he led the league in home runs and runs batted in. He lost the 1944 MVP award by one vote to the Cardinals' Marty Marion. That season, Nicholson was such a threat at the plate that he was walked with the bases loaded. On July 23, New York Giants manager Mel Ott ordered Nicholson passed in a game the Giants led, 12-9. The gamble worked as the Giants won the game, 12-10.

Nicholson spent 10 years patrolling the outfield at Wrigley Field and gained legions of fans for his ability to play the "sun field" in right. He came to Chicago after playing for former Cubs star Kiki Cuyler, who was managing in the minors at Chattanooga. Cuyler tutored Nicholson and overhauled his batting stance. Soon, the young slugger led the league in home runs and RBI. Midway through the 1939 season, the Cubs purchased his contract for $35,000. Nicholson homered in his first game.

But by 1948, Nicholson's power numbers had faded and he often complained of fatigue. Doctors discovered he had diabetes. The Cubs traded him to the Phillies prior to the 1949 season. He played five more years in the league, mostly as a pinch hitter. He returned to his Maryland farm where he died in 1996.

Claude Passeau
Pitcher, 1939-1947

Passeau was a dominating pitcher who joined the Cubs just as the team hit the skids. Passeau won 20 games in 1940, when the team started a streak of five straight losing seasons.

Passeau had a reputation of intimidating batters by throwing inside. Cincinnati Reds slugger Hank Sauer, who would later play for the Cubs, remembered a run-in with the pitcher in 1942. "In the second game of the season against the Cubs, I came up against Passeau and hit a home run into the centerfield seats. As I'm rounding second base, he yells at me, `You bush son of a bitch. You're going down next time.' And sure enough, the next time up, down I go. And the next time after that. He looked at me on the ground and said, `Try hitting it that way.'"

Passeau was big on the number 13. He claimed it was his lucky number. He wore it on the back of his jersey, it was his license plate number and his home address was 113 London Street. He also was big with the bat. He hit 15 home runs in his career, including a grand slam in 1941.

Despite pitching the entire 1945 season with bone chips in his elbow, Passeau declined surgery and put up a 17-9 record, leading the league with five shutouts. The three-time All-Star saved his best pitching effort for the postseason. In Game 3 of the World Series against Detroit, Passeau threw a one-hitter and beat the Tigers, 3-0. It would be his last season of regular work. The next two years, he pitched mainly in relief.

Passeau spent two more years managing in the Cubs' minor league system before returning to Mississippi, where he ran a John Deere dealership for many years.

Nicholas "Dom" Dallessandro
Outfielder, 1940-1944; 1946-1947

Dom Dallessandro was a superb hitter in the minor leagues. In six seasons, he never hit below .300. He won the 1939 batting crown of the Pacific Coast League with a .368 average, which spurred the Cubs to bring him to the majors. But Dallessandro soon learned why they call it the major leagues. Even with the wartime shortage of pitchers, Dallessandro managed only one season with better than a .290 average. He was an everyday player in only one of his seven years with the Cubs. He served as the team's fourth outfielder and primary pinch-hitter. Dallessandro's best season was 1941 when he had 36 doubles and 85 RBI. His year of military service in 1945 cost him the chance to play on a pennant winner and he returned to the minor leagues after the 1947 season.

Lou Novikoff
Outfielder, 1941-1944

Lou Novikoff was supposed to be the second coming of Rogers Hornsby, but instead of becoming a gate attraction during the war years, Novikoff became a footnote in Cubs history.

In the minor leagues, Novikoff won four consecutive batting titles. And in 1939, he was named minor league Player of the Year by *The Sporting News*. In 1941, the Cubs shelled out $100,000 and trumpeted his arrival in Chicago .

Novikoff soon took the nickname "Mad Russian" for his eccentric play. He was a terrible defensive outfielder who refused to go near the ivy-covered walls at Wrigley, a real liability in fielding the long ball. He once stole third base with the bases loaded, later telling an exasperated Cubs manager Jimmie Wilson, "I know it was a dumb thing to do, but I had such a good jump on the pitcher. I just couldn't resist." On top of everything else, his hitting fell apart. His wife, Esther, would sit in the stands when Novikoff came to bat and yell, "Strike the bum out!" It was supposed to inspire him. It didn't.

After four years with the Cubs, Novikoff was sent back to the minors. He played another six years before returning to California and working briefly as a longshoreman. He died of lung disease in 1970 at age 54.

Hiram "Hi" Bithorn
Pitcher, 1942-1943; 1946

Hi Bithorn was Puerto Rican. His catcher, Chico Hernandez, was Cuban. Together, they formed the first Latino battery in the major leagues.

Bithorn had a career year in 1943. He won 18 games and led the league with seven shutouts. But he became known as much for his fast temper as his fastball. During a game in Brooklyn, Dodgers manager Leo Durocher taunted Bithorn relentlessly. Instead of throwing toward the plate, Bithorn wheeled and fired the ball toward Durocher, narrowly missing his head.

Bithorn was drafted into military service in 1944 and missed two full seasons. When he returned, he was overweight and out of shape. In 1946, he went 6-5 and was sold to the Pirates. After two games for the White Sox in 1947, his major-league career was over.

Bithorn died under mysterious circumstances in 1952. He was travelling in Mexico when he was shot and killed by a policeman. He had been arrested for attempting to sell his American car for $350 without proper papers. On the way to the police station, a struggle ensued and Bithorn was shot. He died on the way to a hospital with $2,000 cash in his pocket. As he lay dying, Bithorn claimed that he was on a secret mission for a Communist cell. The policeman was charged with murder and sent to prison.

In 1963, Bithorn was elected to the Latin Baseball Hall of Fame. The stadium in San Juan, Puerto Rico, is named in his honor.

Hank Wyse
Pitcher, 1942-1947

Hank Wyse was the Cubs' only 20-game winner during the war years.

Wyse was a sinkerball pitcher who grew up in Arkansas of Cherokee descent. He claimed the hot Southern summers made him a better pitcher by teaching him to pace himself. On the mound, he had to wear a corset under his uniform because he injured his back in the minor leagues and reinjured it falling off a ladder in Chicago.

Wyse had his best year during the Cubs' championship season of 1945. He threw a one-hitter against Pittsburgh and ended the season with 22 wins. However, in Game 2 of the World Series against Detroit, he gave up a two-run homer to slugger Hank Greenberg and lost the game, 4-1. During the off-season, Wyse underwent back surgery. He came back to win 14 games in 1946, but the Cubs released him after the 1947 season. Wyse bounced between the major and minor leagues for another four years before retiring in 1951. He settled in Oklahoma, working as an electrician and raising championship hunting dogs.

Harry "Peanuts" Lowrey
Outfielder, 1942-1943; 1945-1949

Harry Lee Lowrey, nicknamed "Peanuts" as a baby, grew up near the movie lots in southern California. He spent his summers playing with cast members from the "Our Gang" comedies and had several roles as a child actor himself. As he grew older, he became a baseball player who, like so many minor leaguers, got his break when so many major-league players went off to war.

Lowrey was a versatile outfielder capable of playing several positions. But after two years with the Cubs, the war called him, too. When he returned in 1945, he had added some weight and produced a career-high 89 RBI.

In 1949, Lowrey was part of a trade that brought slugger Hank Sauer from the Reds to the Cubs. Sauer gave Chicago a true power threat and was named the league's most valuable player of 1952.

Lowrey eventually landed in St. Louis, where he became one of the league's premier pinch-hitters. After a final season with the Phillies in 1955, he began a 20-year career as a minor-league manager and major-league coach, known for his ability to steal the other team's signs. Lowrey also returned to the movies, appearing in several baseball films, including one with a future president, Ronald Reagan.

**Phil Cavarretta and Stan Hack
Polo Grounds, 1945**

By 1945, team captain Phil Cavarretta and third baseman Stan Hack were the lone holdovers from the 1938 title team, but the Cubs were up for another run at the championship.

The two veterans had the highest batting averages of their careers in 1945. Hack, 35, batted .323 in his last season as a regular. Cavarretta, 28, hit .355, won the batting title and was named the league's most valuable player. The team reached the World Series, but lost to the Tigers. Cubs fans would wait two decades to witness another pennant chase.

Both Cavarretta and Hack went on to manage the Cubs during an era marked by mediocre players and front-office mismanagement. The club had a history of acquiring too many players past their prime and trading too many players who became stars elsewhere.

In July 1951, Cavarretta inherited a last-place team from Frankie Frisch. In three seasons, his best finish was fifth. When he openly complained that the team lacked talent, Cavarretta was replaced by Hack in 1954. Hack produced no better than a sixth-place finish in 1955.

Hank Borowy
Pitcher, 1945-1948

Hank Borowy became the pivotal pitcher of the Cubs' 1945 championship season.

Borowy was pitching for the New York Yankees in July 1945, when he gave up a game-winning grandslam to the Tigers. Yankees general manager Larry McPhail was so irate, he immediately put Borowy on waivers. The Cubs, badly needing a pitcher for their pennant chase, claimed him.

The pencil-thin right-hander was just what the Cubs needed. He went 11-2 down the stretch and helped pitch the Cubs to the National League pennant. Borowy ended the season with 21 victories and led the league

with a 2.65 ERA. He won Game 1 of the World Series against Detroit, 9-0. He lost Game 5, but came back the next day to throw four innings of scoreless relief as the Cubs rallied to win Game 6 and even the Series. Amazingly, Cubs manager Charlie Grimm sent Borowy to the mound again two days later for Game 7, but the pitcher was out of gas. He didn't make it out of the first inning as the Tigers coasted to a 9-3 win and the title.

A chronic problem with blisters on his pitching hand shortened Borowy's career. The Cubs traded him to the Phillies in 1949 and he retired two years later. He returned to New Jersey and began a career in real estate.

Roy Smalley
Shortstop, 1948-1953

Roy Smalley got rave reviews for his diving stops and ability to cover ground. He reached balls that most shortstops never saw. Unfortunately, his penchant for throwing the ball into the stands ruined the effect.

His first three years in Chicago, Smalley led all National League shortstops in errors. He also was weak at the plate. Smalley was a career .227 hitter who never batted higher than .250 in any of ten major-league seasons. Cubs fans booed him constantly.

In 1950, Smalley briefly produced some offense for the Cubs. He hit 21 homers and drove in 85 runs, but he also led the league in strike-outs. A broken ankle early in 1951 severely hobbled Smalley and he was never an everyday player again. The Cubs traded him to the Braves in 1954. He later spent three seasons with the Phillies before returning to the minors for two years.

Andy Pafko
Outfielder, 1943-1951

Andy Pafko's rifle arm and booming bat kept him in the major leagues for 17 years. The Cubs traded him away after half of them.

In his first major-league game, Pafko knocked out four hits. The next year, he was the Cubs' starting centerfielder and led the league in assists, gunning down 24 baserunners. Word spread quickly not to challenge the rookie's arm.

Pafko also became the Cubs' best run producer. In 1945, he drove in 110 runs, third-best in the league. A versatile player, Pafko was nicknamed "Handy Andy" by Cubs manager Charlie Grimm for his ability to play wherever needed. In 1948, he was moved to third base and delivered 26 home runs and 101 RBI for the last-place Cubs. When he added another 36 home runs in 1950, Cubs fans had a new idol. But their love affair was short lived as Pafko was traded in June 1951 to Brooklyn in an eight-player deal. Fans were outraged. The feeble play of the newly acquired players only added insult to their collective injury.

Pafko spent the rest of his career with Brooklyn and Milwaukee and played on three pennant-winning teams. He retired after the 1959 season.

Frankie Frisch
Manager, 1949-1951

When the team got off to a lousy start in 1949, the Cubs' front office decided to make a change. They booted long-time manager Charlie Grimm and replaced him with Frankie Frisch, who had previously managed the St. Louis Cardinals for five years and the Pittsburgh Pirates for seven. In his 12 years as a manager, Frisch's teams had only three losing seasons.

As a player, Frisch was known for his hustle on the field. As a manager, he was known as aggressive and argumentative. He loved to challenge umpires and was frequently thrown out of games. Perhaps it was less painful than staying around to witness the Cubs' poor play. Despite the slugging of Hank Sauer and Andy Pafko, the Cubs' pitching staff doomed all chance of success. It was so bad that during Frisch's tenure, no Cubs pitcher won more than 12 games in a single season. With the Cubs record at 35-45 in late July 1951, Frisch resigned and was replaced by Phil Cavarretta.

Philip K. Wrigley
Owner, 1932-1977

No owner had a more lasting impact on the Cubs than Philip K. Wrigley, whose tenure was marked by four decades of decay. Wrigley's father left him a dynasty, but within a decade, the son turned the Cubs franchise into a perennial cellar-dweller.

Philip Wrigley had none of his famous father's flair for promotion and showmanship. He disliked being photographed and rarely appeared in public. He refused television and radio interviews, although he would occasionally speak to a newspaper reporter. He was content to run the family gum business and tinker with antique automobiles at his estate in Lake Geneva, Wisconsin. When questioned about his aversion to publicity, Wrigley replied, "I have decided that I am a very unimpressive man."

The last ten years he owned the Cubs, Wrigley never attended a single game. He did, however, apply various business philosophies to the club. He commissioned psychological tests for players to determine why the team played so poorly. He paid for marketing studies to find out what fans wanted. And in 1961, he experimented with the idea of using multiple managers in one season, a concept that came to be called the College of Coaches. Although he could be generous with players in need and fiercely loyal to employees, Philip Wrigley's ownership of the Cubs was marked by a revolving door of managers and executives. The only constant was lousy results.

For all his efforts, Wrigley was perpetually criticized in public and in the press. In 1977, he told the New York Times, "My gum company made a $40 million profit last year and I can't get the financial writers to say a word about it. But I fire a manager and everybody shows up."

Wrigley abhorred the prospect of lights at Wrigley Field as much as the arrival of free agency in baseball. His stubborn refusal to meet Bill Madlock's contract demands chased the two-time batting champion out of town after the 1976 season. It was yet another instance of the Cubs losing star players to other teams and the most glaring example of an organization without a comprehensive plan. Under Wrigley's tenure, the Cubs were always rebuilding.

Philip K. Wrigley died in 1977 at the age of 82. The ownership of the team was left to his family, who sold the Cubs to the Tribune Company in 1981. The sale ended more than 60 years of Wrigley ownership of the Chicago Cubs.

Ransom "Randy" Jackson
Third baseman, 1950-1955; 1959

Ransom Jackson was a two-time All-Star who hit 84 home runs in five years with the Cubs. More importantly, the third baseman was a favorite of female fans. His nickname: "Handsome Ransom."

Cubs manager Frankie Frisch roundly criticized Jackson for not being more of a "holler" guy, but that wasn't Jackson's style. Jackson was a steady, if unspectacular, infielder.

Following the 1955 season, Jackson was traded to the Brooklyn Dodgers, where he backed up Jackie Robinson and Pee Wee Reese as a reserve infielder. He became the answer to a trivia question when he hit the last home run for the Dodgers before the team left for Los Angeles. Jackson rejoined the Cubs briefly in 1959, before retiring to a career in the insurance business.

Hank Sauer
Outfielder, 1949-1955

With the Cubs stuck at the bottom of the standings, slugger Hank Sauer's majestic home runs became the club's best drawing card of the early 1950's.

Sauer came from the Reds in one of the few trades of the era that benefitted Chicago. His first 15 days with the Cubs, Sauer hit nine home runs and became an instant fan favorite. Knowing their new hero smoked a pipe, Cubs fans began throwing bags of tobacco onto the field whenever Sauer hit a ball over the outfield wall.

Over the next six seasons, Sauer hit 171 home runs for the Cubs. In 1952, he produced 37 home runs and drove in 121 runs. He led the league in both categories and was named its most valuable player. Sauer also became the first Cubs' player to hit three home runs in a game for a second time. Ironically, both times it was against the Phillies' Curt Simmons.

Sauer's last big year was 1954 when he hit 41 home runs and 103 RBI. Two years later, the Cubs traded him to St. Louis for outfielder Pete Whisenant, who batted .239 and was gone after a single season. Sauer played parts of four seasons, primarily with the Giants, before retiring early in the 1959 season.

Dee Fondy
First baseman, 1951-1957

To describe Dee Fondy as a streaky hitter doesn't fully capture his reputation at the plate. Cubs personnel director Wid Mathews, who had plenty of practice evaluating bad ballplayers, probably said it best. He called Fondy "the worst-looking .300 hitter I ever saw."

Fondy replaced the aging Phil Cavarretta at first base in 1952 and batted .300. He batted .309 in 1953. The numbers don't reveal how wildly inconsistent he was. Fondy could look clueless for several at bats, then produce a game-winning hit. Never more than a mediocre fielder, his batting average began to drop and early in 1957, he was traded to Pittsburgh. After a year with the Reds, Fondy returned to the Pacific Coast League for one final season. He retired in 1959.

Joe Garagiola
Catcher, 1953-1954

He played 137 games for the Cubs, but Joe Garagiola is best known for his career off the diamond.

Garagiola started playing baseball as a catcher for his hometown St. Louis Cardinals. At age 20, he played a key role in the 1946 World Series, getting four hits in Game 4. But most of the time, Garagiola played a backup role and St. Louis traded him in 1951. Over the next three years, he played for three different teams. Midway through 1953, Garagiola joined the Cubs. He was gone the following year.

Garagiola's fame came off the field, as a broadcaster. In 1955, he returned to St. Louis to help broadcast Cardinals games. In 1961, he became the voice of NBC's *Game of the Week*, working with Tony Kubec and Vin Scully for 28 seasons. And from 1969 to 1973, he hosted *The Today Show* for NBC.

Garagiola also was a popular emcee on the banquet circuit for many years, regaling listeners with humorous anecdotes about the major leagues. Garagiola was a founding member of a group that assists retired major-league ballplayers.

Chuck Connors
First baseman, 1951

Like Joe Garagiola, Kevin Joseph Connors gained far greater fame off the baseball diamond. As Chuck Connors, he became the star of the popular television western, *The Rifleman*.

Connors, who stood six-foot-five, started his career playing professional basketball with the Boston Celtics. But he played little and scored less. The Brooklyn Dodgers signed him to a baseball contract, but he ended up in the Pacific Coast League. The Cubs recalled him in the middle of the 1951 season, but Connors produced only two home runs and averaged .239 in 66 games. The Cubs sent him back to the minors.

In the offseason, Connors was offered a bit part in a movie starring Spencer Tracy and Katherine Hepburn. The opportunity led Connors, 31, to quit baseball and pursue an acting career. His big break came in 1957 when he was signed to play Lucas McCain in the *Rifleman* series, a lead role he played for six years. He also starred in a second series, *Branded*, which ran for two seasons. Connors appeared in numerous television and movie roles over the next three decades, including the highly acclaimed mini-series *Roots* in 1977.

Ernie Banks
Shortstop, 1953-1961

Six years after Jackie Robinson broke baseball's color barrier with the Brooklyn Dodgers, 22-year old Ernie Banks became the first black player for the Chicago Cubs.

As a ballplayer, Banks was the original "natural" whose unrehearsed talent carried him to the major leagues. Banks never played a day in the minor leagues. His high school didn't even field a baseball team. Instead he ran track, played football and averaged 20 points a game on the school's basketball team.

Banks grew up poor in Dallas, the oldest son of a former Negro League catcher and pitcher. As a youngster, his father had to bribe him with spare change to play catch in the family's backyard. But in 1948, at age 17, Banks signed to play with the Amarillo Colts, a travelling black semi-pro baseball team, where he was spotted by a scout for the Kansas City Monarchs. Banks made the leap to the Negro American League in 1950, playing shortstop for the Monarchs. But his baseball career was interrupted by a two-year hitch in the military.

When he returned from overseas in 1953, Banks re-joined the Monarchs, where he hit .380 with 23 home runs. A manager in the Cubs' farm system saw Banks play a game in Columbus, Georgia, and notified team officials, who dispatched a pair of scouts. As it happened, Banks was soon to play in an all-star game at Comiskey Park. Fearing another team would sign him, the Cubs acted quickly.

On September 8, 1953, the Cubs purchased Banks and a pitcher from the Monarchs for $35,000. On September 17, Banks played shortstop for the Cubs for the first time. It would be one of many firsts for Ernie Banks.

Eddie Miksis
Infielder, 1951-1956

Unable to crack the Dodgers' veteran infield, Eddie Miksis was traded to the Cubs in a multi-player deal that sent popular Andy Pafko to Brooklyn. The trade didn't help improve Miksis or the Cubs.

Miksis missed almost half the 1952 season with a twisted knee, but like other Cubs players of the early 1950's, he played because the team didn't have anyone else. A lifetime .236 hitter, Miksis had little power. The arrival of infielders Ernie Banks and Gene Baker forced Miksis to move to the outfield in 1955, where he produced nine home runs and drove in 41 runs, both career highs. Following the 1956 season, Miksis was traded to the Cardinals. He played two final seasons with three teams before retiring after the 1958 season.

Warren Giles, Stan Hack, Sam Jones and Clyde McCullough
Wrigley Field, 1955

Pitcher Sam Jones liked to do things the hard way. On May 12, 1955, in the top of the ninth inning against Pittsburgh, he walked the first three hitters and loaded the bases. He then struck out the next three batters, preserving his no-hitter. It was the first no-hitter by a Cubs pitcher in 38 years. Jones is shown in this photo being congratulated by National League President Warren Giles, Cubs manager Stan Hack and catcher Clyde McCullough.

Jones possessed an excellent fastball and a devastating curve ball and when he could harness his talent, he was one of the league's dominant pitchers. But he had a problem with control. In 1955 and 1956, he led the league in strike-outs and walks. His no-hitter came in the same year that his 20 losses led the league.

Because he was erratic, teams often gave up on him. Known as "Toothpick Sam" because he pitched with a toothpick in his mouth, Jones was frequently traded. He pitched for seven teams in 12 seasons. In 1959, with the San Francisco Giants, he led the league with 21 wins and a 2.83 ERA. Jones died of cancer in 1971 at age 45.

Gene Baker
Second baseman, 1953-1957

Only a pulled muscle kept Gene Baker from becoming the Cubs' first black player.

Baker spent four seasons with the Cubs' top farm team in the Pacific Coast League. He was a superb shortstop and was being groomed to take Roy Smalley's place in Chicago. But then the Cubs signed shortstop Ernie Banks, who along with Baker, joined the team on September 14, 1953. Three days later, Banks was in the Cubs starting lineup while Baker sat on the bench nursing a pulled rib-cage muscle. The Cubs later asked Baker to move to second because they wanted to keep Banks at shortstop.

As the team's only two black players, Baker and Banks were roommates on the road and became inseparable off the field. Baker, 28, advised the younger Banks on the finer points of playing shortstop. For the next three seasons, the Cubs had their finest double-play tandem since Billy Jurges and Billy Herman in the 1930's. Both Banks and Baker had excellent range. Many of their errors resulted simply from getting to balls that no other infielder could have reached. In 1955, they played the entire 154-game season together. It appeared the Cubs' infield was set for the next decade.

Early in 1957, Baker was moved to third base to make room for a rookie second baseman named Casey Wise. One month later, Baker was moved again, this time to Pittsburgh in a deal for slugger Dale Long. Wise would play 43 games for the Cubs, bat .179 and be gone by season's end. Six different players would play second base over the next seven seasons. Only the arrival of Glenn Beckert in 1965 would provide stability.

With the Pirates, Baker suffered a serious knee injury in 1957 that effectively ended his career. He played 42 games for Pittsburgh before retiring in 1961. He later managed and was a scout in the Pirates organization.

Ernie Banks
Polo Grounds, 1957

Ernie Banks redefined the role of shortstop. Three decades before the arrival of Cal Ripken Jr., major league shortstops were valued for their gloves, not their bats. But Banks' unique combination of defense and power broke the mold.

Banks joined the Cubs in 1953 and hit .314 in ten games. He was so impressive that the Cubs traded veteran shortstop Roy Smalley and gave Banks the everyday job. His first full season, Banks hit 19 home runs and knocked in 79 runs. More importantly, he was strong defensively, teaming with rookie second baseman Gene Baker to create the league's premier defensive tandem. Although prone to errors early in his career, Banks worked hard to improve his defense and in 1960, he won a Gold Glove award.

In his second season, Banks' offensive numbers exploded. He hit .295 and drove in 117 runs. His 44 home runs were the most by a Cubs player in 25 years and set a record for shortstops. By 1957, when he hit 43 homers and knocked in 102 runs, Banks was a superstar in a league that included Willie Mays and Henry Aaron. And he was just getting started.

Walt "Moose" Moryn
Outfielder, 1956-1960

Walt Moryn was a "throw-in" from Brooklyn in the trade that sent Cubs outfielder Ransom Jackson to the Dodgers.

At 30 years old, Moryn joined the Cubs as the regular right-fielder and blossomed into a longball threat. He might have been slow-footed, but he possessed a strong arm and led the league's outfielders with 18 assists in his first season with Chicago.

At the plate, Moryn was equally strong. In 1956, he hit 23 home runs. In 1957, he knocked in 88 runs. And in 1958, he made the All-Star team after hitting 26 home runs, including three in one game against his old team, the Dodgers. Moryn was a favorite of the Wrigley faithful, who yelled "Moose" whenever he stepped to the plate.

Following a down year in 1959, Moryn was traded to the Cardinals early in 1960. He was released after the 1961 season. Moryn later returned to Chicago and worked for Montgomery Wards.

Myron "Moe" Drabowsky
Pitcher, 1956-1960

Moe Drabowsky spent 17 seasons pitching in the major leagues, but may be best remembered for his antics in the bullpen.

A native of Poland, Drabowsky caught the eye of Cubs scouts when he threw a no-hitter while pitching for tiny Trinity College in Connecticut. The Cubs were so desperate for pitching help that they gave Drabowsky a $50,000 signing bonus. Only 21, Drabowsky immediately joined the Cubs and went 2-4 for the rest of the year. In 1957, he won 13 games, including a one-hitter against the Pirates. But he soon developed arm trouble and struggled through the next three seasons.

In 1961, the Cubs gave up on Drabowsky and shipped him to the Braves. He was moved to the bullpen, then became a nomad, pitching for seven teams over the next 12 seasons.

With time on his hands, Drabowsky became famous for his practical jokes. During a game, he would use the bullpen phone to call the other bullpen and order pitchers to begin throwing. He would also order take-out food be delivered to the dugout. And while with the Kansas City Athletics, Drabowsky called up teammates in the offseason and pretended to be team owner Charley Finley. He'd insult them with a low-ball contract offer and tell them to take it or leave it before hanging up the phone. Generally, his off-beat antics kept his team loose.

Drabowsky's shining moment on the mound came in 1966 with Baltimore. In Game 1 of the World Series against the Los Angeles Dodgers, he threw six innings of scoreless relief and struck out 11 to get the victory. In 1969, he won 11 games, all in relief, for the expansion Kansas City Royals. Drabowsky finished his career with the White Sox in 1972. He later returned to baseball and worked as a coach with the White Sox.

Dale Long
First baseman, 1957-1959

Dale Long is best known for hitting a home run in eight straight games while with the Pittsburgh Pirates.

Long rejected a football career with the Green Bay Packers because he figured a baseball career would last longer. In 1956, he hit 27 home runs for the Pirates, including his record-setting string of eight straight. It remains the major league record, tied only by the Yankees' Don Mattingly and Seattle's Ken Griffey, Jr.

Long was traded to the Cubs early in 1957 and hit 21 home runs with a .298 average. The next year, he was one of five Cubs to hit 20 or more home runs for a total of 182 homers, then the Cubs' single-season team record. But all that offense didn't stop the Cubs from going 72-82 and finishing fifth.

When Long's hitting dropped off the next year, he was traded to the Giants. After playing with three teams in four years, he retired after the 1963 season. He worked briefly as a minor-league umpire before moving to Florida in 1978 and joining the minor leagues' governing body. Long died of cancer in 1991 at age 64.

George Altman
Outfielder, 1959-1962; 1965-1967

George Altman was a gifted all-around athlete whose size and power should have made him a star in Chicago.

Altman was signed by the Cubs after playing one season with the Kansas City Monarchs of the Negro Leagues. During spring training of 1959, the Cubs noticed his towering home runs and brought him to Chicago, eventually making him the everyday centerfielder. In 1961, Altman had a huge year, batting .303 with 27 home runs and 96 RBI. In 1962, he hit .318 and added another 22 home runs.

Desperate for pitching help in 1963, the Cubs traded Altman to the Cardinals for pitcher Larry Jackson. The Cubs got a pitcher who would win 52 games over the next three years. The Cardinals got a player who missed Wrigley Field.

In St. Louis, Altman tried to tailor his swing for Busch Stadium's short right-field porch, but the result was a huge drop in run production. By the time Altman joined the Cubs in 1965, after one sub-par season with the Mets, he was 32 and past his prime. A series of nagging injuries limited him to part-time duty. He never regained his previous form and following the 1967 season, he left to play baseball in Japan.

There, Altman became a star. In seven seasons, he hit 205 home runs and batted .305. In 1975, at age 42, Altman returned to Chicago and became a commodities trader at the Board of Trade.

Ernie Banks
1958 All-Star Game, Baltimore

Shortstop Ernie Banks is the greatest player never to have played in a World Series.

From 1955 to 1960, Banks hit more home runs than any player in either league, more than Mickey Mantle, Willie Mays or Henry Aaron. He excelled in the field and at the plate. Banks was selected to 14 All-Star teams at a time when the National League dominated the mid-season classic. Banks also set club records for games played, total bases and extra base hits, records that stand today. His production and longevity earned him the nickname "Mr. Cub."

Banks was elected to the Hall of Fame in 1977. In 1982, he became the first Cubs player to have his number, 14, retired. Today it flies on a flag over Wrigley Field.

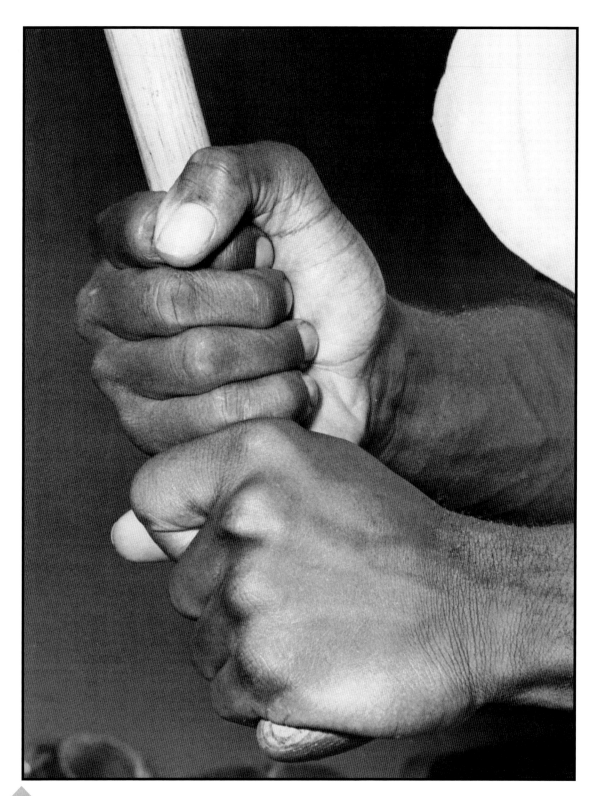

Ernie Banks' batting grip

At first glance, Ernie Banks didn't look like a slugger. He stood six-foot-one and was thin as a rail. But at the plate, Banks took a position that put runs on the board.

Banks liked to hold his bat high above his head and wiggle it, anticipating the pitch. But he always waited for the last possible moment to swing. One opponent said he "hits the ball right out of the catcher's mitt." Banks' secret was his quick, powerful wrists. A teammate once remarked, "He has wrists right up to his armpits." In 19 seasons with the Cubs, those wrists produced 512 home runs and drove in 1,636 runs.

Billy Williams
Outfielder, 1959-1974

Billy Williams was a steady, often spectacular, outfielder whose All-Star career was overshadowed by those of others.

Williams built a reputation on consistency and dependability. He drove in at least 90 runs a year for 10 straight seasons. He hit 20-plus home runs in 13 of his 14 full seasons with the Cubs. And he once played in 1,117 consecutive games.

Williams was named to the National League All-Star team four times.

The Cubs discovered Williams when they sent a scout to Alabama to evaluate Tommie Aaron, Hank's younger brother and Billy's teammate. Most of the time in the minors, though, Williams was the only black player on the team. On the road, he had to stay with a black family. Restaurants often refused to serve him. His fourth year in the minors, Williams was so homesick that he left the team and returned to Mobile. Buck O'Neil, a former Negro Leagues star who scouted for the Cubs, convinced him to return.

Back in Chicago, Williams worked hard to overcome his reputation as a poor defensive outfielder because the Cubs needed his bat in the line-up. Williams rewarded the team's confidence by being named the 1961 NL Rookie of the Year. But the hoopla surrounding Yankee sluggers Mickey Mantle and Roger Maris, and their chase of Babe Ruth's homerun mark, stole the headlines of the day.

Even the arrival of a player as talented as Williams didn't immediately make the Cubs contenders. Chicago remained in the cellar another six seasons. However, the trio of Williams, Banks and Ron Santo gave the club a nucleus of sluggers on which to build.

Throughout his 18 years in the major leagues, Williams let his bat do the talking. Teammate Ernie Banks said, "Billy didn't talk much. Billy just played." And play he did. In 1964, Williams batted .312 and made the All-Star team. In 1965, he hit .315 and led the Cubs in every offensive category. In 1970, he led the league in hits and runs scored. In recognition of his talents, the Cubs made Williams the team's first $100,000 player.

Ernie Banks and Warren Giles
Wrigley Field, 1960

Ernie Banks was named the National League's most valuable player in 1958 and 1959. During that time, he hit 92 home runs, drove in 272 runs and batted .308. Banks was the first NL player to win the award twice in a row. Here, National League president Warren Giles presents the 1959 award to Banks at Wrigley Field.

Ron Santo
Third baseman, 1960-1973

Ron Santo is the greatest third baseman in Cubs history. He won five Gold Glove awards and was named to 10 All-Star teams. For eight years in a row, he hit at least 25 home runs a year. In four, he drove in more than 100 runs. He played hard and he played hurt and no one else played the hot corner as long or as well.

Santo was a leader on and off the field and so at age 25, he was named team captain. Santo expected his teammates to play all-out and when they didn't, the outspoken young captain let them know it.

In the ill-fated season of 1969, Santo had one of his best years. He led the team with 29 home runs and 123 RBI. His habit of clicking his heels together after a Cubs win delighted the fans, who thought the team was headed for a championship. But when the team faded in September, and finished second to the Mets, Santo's charming habit was ridiculed in the Chicago press. He became the whipping boy for the team's failures. Santo was an emotional player who wanted to win more than anything and he couldn't hide his feelings, admitting, "I just don't give a good act."

Late in his career, Santo announced he was a diabetic. It was the only thing he had kept hidden from the public.

In 1973, the Cubs finished fifth and when the season was over, Cubs owner Philip K. Wrigley decided wholesale changes were needed. He traded the team's veteran players, including Santo, who joined the White Sox for one final season. Santo retired a year later with 342 home runs and 2,254 hits. During his 14 years with the Cubs, Santo had invested wisely and had become a wealthy man. In 1990, he joined WGN as the color man for Cubs radio broadcasts.

**College of Coaches
Spring Training, 1961**

Seeking drastic measures for a dreary team, Cubs owner Philip K. Wrigley tried a novel management approach — the College of Coaches, a group of eight coaches who took turns calling the shots.

Wrigley devised the system because he believed the role of team manager was vastly overrated. But the idea was a disaster. Cubs players never knew who was in charge. Star players like Ernie Banks and Billy Williams were shifted from position to position, depending on the whims of a coach. When the Cubs lost 103 games in 1962 and finished behind the expansion Houston Colt .45's, the experiment was scrapped.

Shown above are the original eight coaches. Starting in the front row, left to right: Elvin Tappe, Goldie Holt, Bobby Adams and Harry Craft. In the back row, left to right: Verlon Walker, Rip Collins, Vedie Himsl and Charlie Grimm.

Ken Hubbs
Second baseman, 1961-1963

Ken Hubbs was what the future looked like.

The Cubs spotted Hubbs in Utah, where he was an all-American kid: a straight-A student, senior class president, a devout Mormon and a star in four sports. Signed by the Cubs, Hubbs spent two years in the minors learning his craft. By Opening Day 1962, he was the Cubs' everyday second baseman.

In 1963, he played 78 consecutive games without an error, establishing a new record for second basemen, since broken. He won a Gold Glove and was named Rookie of the Year. His father, confined to a wheelchair with polio, attended games at Wrigley Field to watch him play.

Tragedy struck in February 1964. Hubbs was killed in a plane crash in his native Utah. Along with a childhood friend, Hubbs, who had his pilot's license less than a month, flew in bad weather. Thousands turned out for his funeral and several Cubs teammates, including Ron Santo and Ernie Banks, served as pallbearers. Hubbs died at 22.

Don Cardwell
Pitcher, 1960-1962

In his first start with the Cubs, pitcher Don Cardwell threw a no-hitter, the first time in major-league history that a pitcher threw a no-hitter immediately following a trade.

The Cubs were playing the Cardinals at Wrigley Field and Cardwell, who had just arrived from the Phillies, was on the mound. Cardwell retired 26 straight batters. Only a walk to the game's second batter kept him from throwing a perfect game. When outfielder Moose Moryn made a diving catch for the final out, the crowd of more than 33,000 charged onto the field in celebration.

The remainder of Cardwell's career was good, though less dramatic. In 1960, he led Cubs' pitchers in strikeouts, with 150. In 1961, he won 15 games and led the league in starts. But his stay in Chicago was brief. After winning only seven games in 1962, Cardwell was traded to the Pirates. He later spent four years with the New York Mets before retiring after the 1970 season.

Dick Ellsworth
Pitcher, 1958-1966

In 1963, Cubs pitcher Dick Ellsworth became the team's first left-handed, 20-game winner in 45 years.

Ellsworth was big and strong, but discovered at a young age that there was more to pitching in the majors than throwing hard. Early on, he got knocked around and lost more than he won. Then he learned to throw a slider. Armed with a new pitch, Ellsworth went from losing 20 games in 1962 to winning 22 in 1963. On June 1, he threw a one-hitter against the Phillies and was named the Comeback Player of the Year. It was the high point of his career.

When the Cubs' record went south the following year, so did Ellsworth's. He won 14 games each of the next two seasons, but by 1966, when the Cubs lost 103 games, 22 belonged to Ellsworth. Following the 1966 season, the big left-hander was traded to the Phillies. Later, he played with a string of bad teams. His only other winning season would be in 1968, when the Boston Red Sox won the American League pennant and Ellsworth contributed 16 wins. He retired after the 1971 season. He returned to Fresno and entered the real estate business.

John "Buck" O'Neil
Coach, 1962-1965

After spending nearly 20 years playing and managing in the Negro Leagues, Buck O'Neil became the first black coach in the major leagues.

As a player, O'Neil was a terrific hitter and an excellent first baseman. He won a batting title in 1946 with a .353 average. In 1948, he became player-manager of the Kansas City Monarchs, winning five pennants in eight years. The Cubs hired O'Neil as a scout in 1955 and shortly afterwards, he helped sign Billy Williams and Lou Brock.

In 1962, the Cubs made O'Neil a coach, a position he held for four years. O'Neil later returned to Kansas City, where he helped establish a museum dedicated to the Negro Leagues. In 1994, he gained a new generation of fans after his featured appearance in Ken Burns' PBS documentary, *Baseball*.

Larry Jackson
Pitcher, 1963-1966

Larry Jackson was a superb pitcher who spent 14 years in the majors, never with a pennant-winning club.

Jackson debuted with St. Louis in 1955 and won 101 games in eight years. He became the workhorse of the Cardinals' pitching staff, four times leading the team in innings-pitched. In 1964, the Cardinals started a run of three World Series appearances, but Jackson was in Chicago with the Cubs. The Cardinals had traded him prior to the 1963 season.

His first year in Chicago, Jackson went 14-18 despite an ERA of 2.55, sixth-best in the National League. The pitcher got almost no run support from the Cubs' anemic offense. In his 18 losses, the Cubs scored a total of 29 runs. Three times, Jackson lost by a score of 1-0.

In 1964, Jackson had the best year of his career. He won 24 games, the most by a Cubs pitcher in 37 years. On June 30, he threw a one-hitter against the Reds at Wrigley Field. Only a single by Pete Rose kept him from throwing a perfect game. But both Jackson and the Cubs struggled the following year.

Early in the 1966 season, Jackson was traded to the Phillies in a deal that brought outfielder Adolfo Phillips and pitcher Ferguson Jenkins to the Cubs. It was one of the few trades that favored the Cubs and it set the stage for the team's resurgence in the late 1960's. For his part, Jackson won another 41 games in three seasons with Philadelphia. He retired after the 1968 season and returned to his native Idaho, where he served four terms in the state legislature. Jackson died of cancer in 1990 at age 59.

Lou Brock
Outfielder, 1961-1964

Lou Brock is the one who got away.

The Cubs signed Brock after the 1959 Pan-American games and sent him to their minor league affiliate in the Class C Northern League. His first year, Brock tore it up and was named player of the year.

The Cubs called up Brock late in 1961, but he got off to a disappointing start, going 1 for 11 at the plate. Still, a strong spring training and a lack of real competition kept Brock, 22, in the starting line-up for 1962.

Two things became clear over the next two seasons. First, Brock was immensely talented and could run like the wind. Second, he misplayed fly balls and frequently threw to the wrong base.

The Cubs' coaches were tough on him, shifting him from centerfield to right field and back. It was clear that Brock was a work in progress, but his raw talent was obvious to everyone who saw him. At least it was obvious to those paying attention. When Brock hit two home runs and a triple, driving in five runs against the St. Louis Cardinals on July 28, 1963, it was duly noted in the opposing dugout. A year later, the Cubs traded Brock to the Cardinals as part of a six-player deal.

In St. Louis, playing for a contender, Brock blossomed. He hit .348 in the second half of the season and ended the year with 14 home runs, 30 doubles and 43 stolen bases. Over the next 15 years, Brock would collect 2,713 hits and lead the National League in stolen bases eight times. His 938 career stolen bases was baseball's all-time record until broken by Rickey Henderson in 1991.

Brock, a four-time All Star, was elected to the Hall of Fame in 1985.

Doug Clemens, Bobby Shantz, Ernie Broglio
Wrigley Field, 1964

These are the three players obtained from St. Louis in the Lou Brock trade:

• Doug Clemens, who'd been a reserve outfielder in St. Louis. Clemens hit .221 his only full season in Chicago. The next year, the Cubs traded him to the Phillies.

• Pitcher Bobby Shantz, the American League's most valuable player in 1952. At the time of the trade, Shantz was 38, well past his prime and used sparingly as a reliever in St. Louis. In Chicago, Shantz threw 11 innings of relief before he was sold to the Phillies in August. He retired two months later.

• Pitcher Ernie Broglio, who led the National League with 21 wins in 1960. With the Cubs, Broglio went 7-19 in parts of three seasons before chronic arm problems forced him to retire in 1966.

In 1979, Cardinals outfielder Lou Brock recorded his 3,000th career hit in a game against the Cubs.

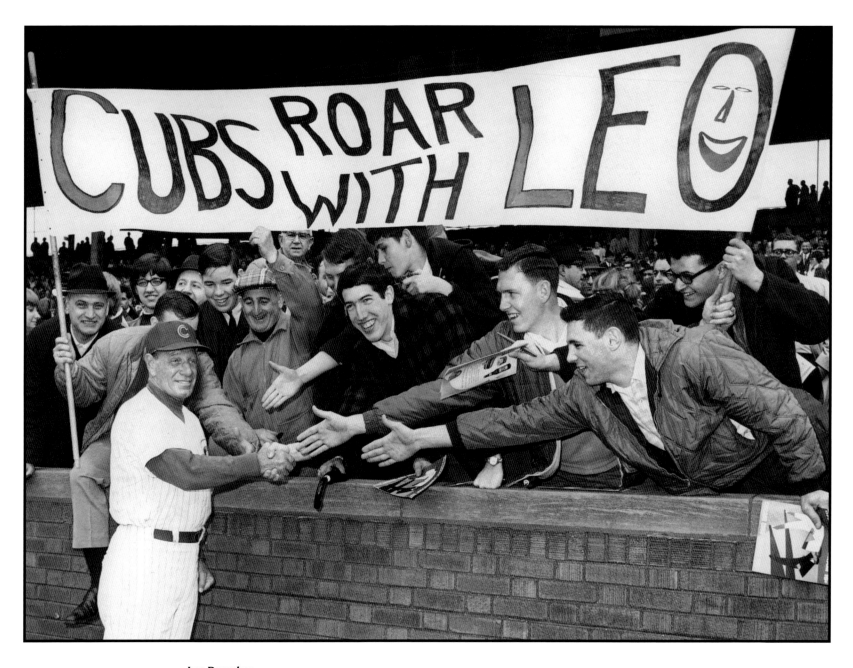

Leo Durocher
Wrigley Field, 1966

The 1966 arrival of Leo Durocher as Cubs manager signaled the beginning of a new era in Cubs baseball. At least for a little while.

The brash Durocher hadn't managed a club in more than a decade, but Cubs owner Philip K. Wrigley was sure the 30-year baseball veteran was the answer for a franchise with two winning seasons in 20 years. Cubs fans were beside themselves with glee. They knew all about "Leo the Lip" and his no-

holds-barred style. They knew he was a loud, abrasive, umpire-baiting egomaniac whose win-at-all-costs attitude would carry a heavy price tag. They were sure it would be a bargain.

In his first press conference, Durocher confirmed his reputation, saying, "I'm not coming here to win popularity contests. And I'm not a nice guy. I haven't mellowed. I'm still the same S.O.B. I always was."

Don Kessinger
Shortstop, 1964-1975

When the Cubs moved Ernie Banks to first base in 1962, they struggled to find a replacement shortstop with a golden glove and a loud bat. In 1964, the club reached into the minors for Don Kessinger, who was good in the field but lacked confidence at the plate. Kessinger's reputation changed when Leo Durocher arrived as manager.

Durocher, himself a former shortstop, tutored the young rookie. He encouraged him to become a switch-hitter, a move that turned things around. Kessinger hit .274 in 1966 and over time, he developed into one of the game's premier shortstops. He was the Cubs' lead-off hitter for most of his career. By getting on base in front of Banks, Billy Williams and Ron Santo, Kessinger twice scored more than 100 runs in a season.

In 11 seasons as the Cubs' everyday shortstop, Kessinger was an All-Star six times. In 1969, he reached base in 41 straight games and led all NL shortstops in fielding percentage. In 1971, he became the first Cubs player since Frank Demaree in 1937 to collect six hits in a game. But the Cubs' failure to win a pennant caused owner Philip K. Wrigley to break up the team and, in 1976, Kessinger was traded. He spent 1½ seasons with the Cardinals before returning to Chicago with the White Sox, where he briefly served as player-manager before resigning during the 1979 season. Kessinger returned to his alma mater, the University of Mississippi, and coached the baseball team for six years before becoming the university's associate athletic director in 1996.

Ferguson Jenkins
Pitcher, 1966-1973; 1982-1983

In an era of outstanding pitchers, Ferguson Jenkins was in a class by himself.

For six straight years between 1967 and 1972, Jenkins won at least 20 games a year. He was often compared with future Hall-of-Fame pitchers Bob Gibson, Juan Marichal and Tom Seaver. But only Jenkins put together six straight.

The Cubs found Jenkins throwing in relief for the Phillies. They acquired him in 1966 and manager Leo Durocher made him a starter. His first season, Jenkins went only 6-8, but he struck out 148 batters in 182 innings, a sign of things to come.

Everything came together for Jenkins his second year with the Cubs. He went 20-13 and led the National League with 20 complete games. In 1968, he began four straight seasons of throwing more than 300 innings a year.

In 1969, Jenkins led the league with 273 strike-outs and in 1970, he set the Cubs' single-season record with 274. In 1971, he was named the NL Cy Young Award winner. Jenkins remains the Cubs' all-time strike-out leader with 2,038.

Jenkins possessed tremendous control. He rarely walked opposing batters. His only weakness was a tendency to give up home runs in bunches. But he was also a victim of the Cubs' poor offense. In 1968, Jenkins went 20-15, but five of the losses were by a score of 1-0.

In 1973, after winning 127 games in six seasons for the Cubs, Jenkins won only 14 games and was traded to the Texas Rangers in a deal that brought Bill Madlock to the Cubs. Jenkins regained his form and won 25 games for the lowly Rangers in 1974. He pitched another nine seasons, but never again won 20 games. Jenkins returned to the Cubs at age 38. He won 20 games over two seasons before retiring after the 1983 season with 284 career wins. In 1991, Jenkins was elected to the Hall of Fame.

Adolfo Phillips
Outfielder, 1966-1969

Outfielder Adolfo Phillips came to Chicago in the trade that brought pitcher Ferguson Jenkins to the Cubs in 1966.

Manager Leo Durocher liked what he saw in Phillips and put him in centerfield, calling him "the next Willie Mays." Sportswriters liked his speed and dubbed him the "Panama Express," a tribute to his homeland. Phillips became a favorite of the Wrigley bleacher bums who loved his flamboyant style.

His first year with the Cubs, Phillips hit 14 home runs and stole 32 bases. His power and speed were just what the team needed. But Phillips was prone to injuries, partly because he liked to crowd the plate, leading pitchers to bean him. Durocher expected Phillips to play hurt and the two were often at odds. Durocher publicly accused Phillips of loafing in an attempt to motivate him. It didn't work.

In 1969, Phillips broke his wrist in spring training and when he returned two months later, his batting average tumbled, his power gone. That June, the Cubs traded him to the expansion Montreal Expos. Two seasons later, Phillips, 29, was out of the majors for good.

Bill Hands
Pitcher, 1966-1972

Bill Hands was part of the kiddie-core pitching staff the Cubs assembled in the late 1960's.

During his first season in Chicago, Hands, who'd been a reliever in San Francisco, failed to finish a single one of 26 starts. But he worked on his endurance and earned his way back into the starting rotation in 1968. Hands, along with Ken Holtzman and Joe Niekro, gave Chicago three starters under the age of 23.

Hands won 16 games in 1968, including four shutouts. His willingness to pitch inside with his fastball allowed him to keep opposing batters off stride, setting the stage for his slider on the outside corner of the plate. This combination produced a career year in 1969. Hands won 20 games, threw 300 innings and his 2.49 ERA was the lowest on the Cubs' staff. But even his success couldn't keep the Mets from blowing by the Cubs in the last month of the season and winning the pennant.

In 1972, after he won only 11 games, the Cubs traded Hands to the Minnesota Twins. He retired in 1975.

Ken Holtzman
Pitcher, 1965-1971; 1978-1979

Ken Holtzman is the only Cubs pitcher to throw two no-hitters in the 20th Century.

The first took place at Wrigley Field on August 20, 1969. The Cubs were playing the Atlanta Braves. Holtzman won 3-0, supported by a team that made some sensational defensive plays. It would be the centerpiece of a season that saw Holtzman throw 33 consecutive scoreless innings.

Holtzman won 17 games for two straight years, but the team remained troubled. Durocher's constant criticism had grown tiresome and several players, including Holtzman, publicly challenged his tactics. Holtzman fell out of favor and his wins fell to just nine in 1971. One of those wins, however, was Holtzman's second no-hitter, against the Cincinnati Reds on June 3.

When the season ended, Holtzman was traded to the Oakland A's, the best team in the American League. Holtzman was the ace the A's needed to put them over the top. He won 77 games in four years and helped pitch the A's to three straight World Series titles. He later pitched for the New York Yankees, but his arm was shot and he won only 12 games in two years. This didn't stop the Cubs from reacquiring Holtzman in 1978. In a colossal blunder, the Cubs traded away reliever Ron Davis, who won 14 games for the Yankees in 1979 and went on to become one of the premier closers in the American League with the Minnesota Twins. Holtzman went 6-12 in two seasons with Chicago and promptly retired.

Joe Niekro
Pitcher, 1967-1969

Joe Niekro won 221 games during 21 years in the majors. Unfortunately for the Cubs, only 24 of those victories came with Chicago.

Niekro was proof that the Cubs could find good young pitchers, they just couldn't keep them. Niekro was 22 when he joined the Cubs. He won 10 games his rookie year, including two shutouts. In 1968, he won another 14.

Early in 1969, however, manager Leo Durocher chose Niekro to relieve against the Pirates. Niekro, a starter, had pitched seven innings only two days earlier. In relief, Niekro gave up a home run to Willie Stargell. Two days later, he was traded to the San Diego Padres.

Niekro became a baseball nomad, pitching for six different teams in the next 19 years. His best seasons came in Houston, where he twice won 20 games. Like his brother Phil, Joe Niekro threw a knuckleball that kept his career alive longer than most. At age 43, Niekro finally made it to his first World Series with the 1987 Minnesota Twins.

Billy Williams and Ernie Banks
1968

The Cubs finished third in 1967 and 1968, their best showings in more than 20 years. In 1968, the so-called "year of the pitcher," sluggers Billy Williams and Ernie Banks combined to hit 62 home runs. As a team, the Cubs led the National League with 130 home runs. In addition, Williams drove in 98 runs, the second highest total in the league. All that offense set the stage for a run at the pennant in 1969.

Randy Hundley
Catcher, 1966-1973; 1976-1977

Catcher Randy Hundley was the Cubs' iron man behind the plate, recognized with a Gold Glove in 1967 and an All-Star appearance in 1969.

Hundley came to the Cubs in the trade that brought pitcher Bill Hands from the Giants. San Francisco had given up on Hundley, partly because he insisted on catching pitches with one hand. Although common today, the approach was considered risky and unorthodox.

But Cubs manager Leo Durocher liked the rookie's take-charge style and made him the everyday catcher in 1966. Hundley agitated opposing batters, challenged umpires and rode herd on the Cubs' young pitching staff. And he played almost every day. Between 1966 and 1969, Hundley caught 612 of the 647 games the Cubs played. He became the first backstop ever to catch 150 games for three straight years.

However, squatting behind the plate for all those games took their toll. In 1970, Hundley tore knee ligaments and missed half the season. In 1971, he twice injured his other knee and missed all but nine games. Hundley was never the same again. When he finally returned in 1972, he was in such pain that he had to have both legs taped from hip to ankle.

Although severely hobbled, Hundley still could call a great game. In 1972, he was behind the plate for the no-hitters thrown by Burt Hooton and Milt Pappas. But his weakened knees crippled his power and his batting average dropped. After the 1973 season, the Cubs traded Hundley to the Minnesota Twins. He struggled to play parts of another two seasons before rejoining the Cubs in 1976 as a player-coach. He appeared in 15 more games before calling it quits. Hundley later managed for three seasons in the minors.

**Ferguson Jenkins
1968**

Before the days of million-dollar salaries, ballplayers moonlighted in the offseason. Pitcher Ferguson Jenkins, who'd been a high school basketball star in Canada, twice toured with the Harlem Globetrotters, traveling all over Canada and the United States. During the games, the six-foot-five pitcher would break into a baseball routine with the Globetrotters' legendary showman Meadowlark Lemon.

Don Kessinger and Glenn Beckert
Shea Stadium, 1969

For nine years, the Cubs' infield was anchored by shortstop Don Kessinger and second baseman Glenn Beckert.

The pair also led off the top of the order, with Kessinger in the lead-off position and Beckert hitting second. Beckert, who liked to choke up on his bat, led the league in fewest strike-outs for five straight years. Three times in his career, he had hitting streaks of 20 or more games. In 1971, he batted .342, the third best in the league.

Cubs fans best remember the duo for their defensive play. Kessinger's range and Beckert's toughness proved a winning combination. Together, they were honored with nine All-Star appearances.

Leo Durocher
Manager, 1966-1972

Manager Leo Durocher may have been the best and worst thing that ever happened to the Chicago Cubs. His old-school style and abrasive personality angered those around him, but he jolted the club out of the doldrums and into contention for the first time in 30 years. Under him, the Cubs finished third in 1967 and 1968, their best showings since 1946.

Durocher was driven to win. It was all he knew or understood. His public goading of players slowly showed results, but as the Cubs began to win, Durocher became even more demanding. The players began to resent the constant criticism they saw in the daily papers. Don Kessinger recalled, "One thing was different about Leo, he didn't believe in private conversations. If he had something to say to you, he'd say it in front of everybody and a lot of guys didn't like that. There were guys who'd listen to his radio show to see if they were playing that day."

Durocher's behavior was tolerated only as long as the Cubs won. In 1969, when the Cubs lost an eight-game lead in the final month of the season, Durocher was blamed. In turn, Durocher called Ferguson Jenkins a "quitter" in a clubhouse meeting, then went AWOL himself in late July. For two days, he stayed away, complaining of an upset stomach. Late in the season, Durocher stopped talking to the press altogether.

In 1970, tensions remained high despite another second-place finish. The Cubs played well on the field, but in the clubhouse, Durocher's tirades grew old. Things came to a head the next year. After a loss to the Houston Astros in late August, Durocher screamed at pitcher Milt Pappas for giving up the winning home run. Veterans Joe Pepitone and Ron Santo told Durocher to lay off, and Santo's teammates had to restrain him from going after Durocher. "Leo the Lip" had lost control of the team.

Philip K. Wrigley took out a full page ad in the local papers telling Cubs fans that he stood behind his manager. And Durocher returned in 1972, under orders to tone it down. But the next year, with the Cubs in fourth place, Durocher was fired mid-season. He managed the Astros for the rest of 1972, but when Houston finished fourth in 1973, he was finally done.

Durocher died in 1991 and was elected to the Hall of Fame in 1994.

Jack Brickhouse
Wrigley Field, 1970

Jack Brickhouse began broadcasting Cubs games on radio in 1942. By the time he was 26, he was calling both the Cubs and the White Sox games on WGN.

In 1948, Brickhouse jumped to television and for the next 34 seasons, his patented call of "hey-hey" echoed from living rooms across Chicago.

The sale of the Cubs to the Tribune Company in 1981 spelled the end of the line for Brickhouse. The new owners hired Harry Caray to call the games on Channel 9. In 1983, Brickhouse received the Ford C. Frick award, presented to distinguished broadcasters at the Hall of Fame.

Ron Santo and Glenn Beckert
Wrigley Field, 1969

During the 1960's, Cubs infielders received ten Gold Glove awards. Third baseman Ron Santo and second baseman Glenn Beckert, who won the 1968 awards for their respective positions, are shown here picking up their hardware the following spring. It was one of five such awards for Santo.

Jim Hickman
Outfielder, 1968-1973

Jim Hickman was the Cubs' super-substitute during the ill-fated pennant chase of 1969.

Hickman's weak hitting kept him out of the starting lineup until the stretch run, when he suddenly became the Cubs' hottest hitter. As pennant hopes wilted in August, Hickman grew even hotter at the plate. He hit 10 home runs and drove in 25 runs in August alone.

In 1970, Hickman had the best year of his career, batting .315 with 32 home runs. In the All-Star game, he drove home Pete Rose, the winning run, in the 12th inning. But Hickman suffered from stomach ulcers and his numbers fell dramatically over the next three seasons. In 1974, at age 36, he was traded to the Cardinals. He played one final season before retiring to his Tennessee farm.

Joe Pepitone
First baseman, 1970-1973

Four times with the Yankees, Joe Pepitone hit 25 or more home runs. He had an arm so strong that he could play first base or the outfield. But Pepitone is probably equally remembered for his long hair, flashy wardrobe and flamboyant personality.

Pepitone was an immediate hit when the Cubs claimed him off waivers in the middle of the 1970 season. He drove in 30 runs in his first 29 games. And when he wasn't playing for the Cubs, he was a regular in the bars on Rush Street. He even opened a nightspot called "Joe Pepitone's Thing."

But the nightlife took its toll and Pepitone's playing time decreased every year. Early in 1972, Pepitone said he was retiring from the Cubs, but soon he was back, followed by mounting bills. He told reporters, "You make $80,000 and you end up spending $100,000 that year. It's the American way of life." The following season he was traded to Atlanta, where he played three games before leaving to play baseball in Japan. In 1978, Pepitone was back in Chicago, broke. He wrote a book, posed for a nude layout, married a Playboy bunny and tried to pay for his two divorces. Pepitone later recalled, "I hustle a buck anyway I can, as long as it's legit. What do I have to offer besides my name and my flaky reputation?" By 1985, he was back in his native New York, where he briefly served time for drug and weapons charges.

Milt Pappas
Pitcher, 1970-1973

Milt Pappas came within one pitch of throwing a perfect game for the Cubs, but had to settle for a no-hitter.

In the middle of the 1970 season, at age 31, Pappas joined the Cubs and went 10-8 over the rest of the year. In 1971, he won 17 games, including a league-leading five shutouts.

But his greatest moment came at Wrigley Field against the San Diego Padres on September 2, 1972. Pappas retired 26 straight batters before walking a pinch-hitter with two outs in the ninth inning. When the next batter popped up to the Cubs' second baseman, Pappas had a no-hitter.

1972 was Pappas' last winning season. In 1973, he went 7-12 and was released. He retired with 209 wins. Pappas is the only pitcher to win 200 games without ever having a 20-win season.

Jose Cardenal
Outfielder, 1972-1977

Cuban-born Jose Cardenal was one of the most colorful players ever to wear a Cubs uniform.

By the time he arrived in Chicago, Cardenal had played for four teams and had three years with at least 35 stolen bases each. He also had a reputation for being lazy and moody. He sometimes appeared to loaf on the field. Some considered him a "hot dog" because of his skin-tight pants and Afro hairstyle. Manager Leo Durocher stationed Cardenal in right field, where he quickly became a fan favorite, especially among the Cubs' Hispanic fans. It also was reported that Cardenal was owner Philip K. Wrigley's favorite player.

His first season with the Cubs, Cardenal hit 17 home runs and stole 25 bases. In 1973, his .303 average led the club. Even when the Cubs finished last in 1974, Cardenal continued to produce. In 1975, he hit .317 and stole 34 bases. In 1976, he collected six hits in a game against the Giants.

In 1977, when Wrigley died, Cardenal was one of the few Cubs players to attend the funeral. Soon, injuries and a change in the Cubs' front office meant less playing time for Cardenal. Outspoken and critical about his reduced role, Cardenal was traded to the Phillies after the 1977 season. He retired after the 1980 season.

Billy Williams
Candlestick Park, 1973

Billy Williams got better with age.

In 1970, at age 32, Williams had the best year of his career. He batted .322 and led the National League in hits and runs scored. His 42 home runs and 129 RBI were his highest ever. He finished second to the Reds' Johnny Bench in balloting for the league's most valuable player.

In 1972, at 34, Williams won the league's batting title with a .333 average. His 37 home runs and 122 RBI were the second best of his career.

After 16 years with the Cubs, Williams was traded to the Oakland A's following the 1974 season. He retired two years later with 426 home runs and 2,711 hits. In 1987, the Cubs retired Williams' uniform number after he was elected to the Hall of Fame.

Andre Thornton
First baseman, 1973-1976

Andre Thornton is another talent that the Cubs gave away.

In 1973, the Cubs traded veteran Joe Pepitone to Atlanta for the 23-year-old Thornton, then playing at Triple A. The Cubs brought Thornton along slowly, but in 1975, his third season with the team, Thornton became the everyday first baseman. He hit .293 that year and led the team with 18 home runs.

The following May, Thornton was traded to the Montreal Expos for pitcher Steve Renko and first baseman-outfielder Larry Biittner. It was a terrible trade for the Cubs. Renko won 10 games his first year and was traded the next. Biittner hit 20 home runs in four years with the team, then was sent to the Reds.

Thornton ended up in Cleveland, where he hit 214 home runs over the next nine years. Although he played for a team that twice lost more than 100 games, Thornton was one of the American League's steadiest sluggers. Twice, he drove in more than 100 runs a season. Three times, he hit more than 30 home runs.

Steve Stone
Pitcher, 1974-1976

When the Cubs traded 14-year veteran Ron Santo to the White Sox in 1973, pitcher Steve Stone was one of four players the team received in return.

Stone won his first five starts for the Cubs and finished the year 8-6. The next year, he won 12 games. But in 1976, he suffered a shoulder injury and won only three games. The next year, Stone signed as a free agent with the White Sox and won 27 games in two years. His greatest season was 1980 with the Baltimore Orioles, when he went 25-7 and won the American League Cy Young Award. One year later, arm problems forced him to retire. Stone returned to Chicago in 1983 to join Harry Caray in the Cubs' television booth.

Burt Hooton
Pitcher, 1971-1975

Pitcher Burt Hooton got off to a fast start with the Cubs, but couldn't keep the wins going.

Hooton joined the Cubs after only half a season in the minors. His second game in Chicago, he struck out 15 New York Mets batters. His next start, the three-time All-American from the University of Texas beat the Mets' Tom Seaver with a two-hit shutout. Hooton was 21.

In 1972, manager Leo Durocher chose Hooton to pitch the second game of the season. On April 16, before a crowd of 9,583 hardy souls who braved a bitterly cold and damp day at Wrigley Field, Hooton threw a no-hitter against the Phillies. Although he walked seven batters, his patented knuckle-curveball baffled the hitters. He ended the season with 11 wins.

But over the next three seasons, Hooton could never regain his rookie form. The Cubs traded him to the Los Angeles Dodgers in 1975. He left Chicago with a record of 32-44. In Los Angeles, Hooton won 112 games over the next ten seasons and pitched in three World Series. He retired in 1985 after a final season with the Texas Rangers and later worked as a pitching coach for the Houston Astros.

Rick Monday
Outfielder, 1972-1976

Rick Monday was the first player chosen in the first free-agent draft in 1965.

The former Arizona State All-American was signed by the Kansas City A's, who six years later traded him to the Cubs for pitcher Ken Holtzman. The trade benefited both teams. Monday became the Cubs' regular centerfielder and Holtzman helped pitch the A's to three straight World Series.

In Chicago, Monday hit three home runs in a game against the Phillies in 1972. The next year, he led the Cubs with 26 home runs. In 1976, batting clean-up, he produced a career-high 32 home runs and drove in 77 runs.

Before the 1977 season, Monday was traded to the Los Angeles Dodgers in a multi-player deal that brought first baseman Bill Buckner and shortstop Ivan DeJesus to Chicago. Monday spent eight years with the Dodgers, mostly as a reserve. He appeared in three World Series before retiring after the 1984 season.

Bill Madlock
Third baseman, 1974-1976

Bill Madlock was a four-time National League batting champion whose stay in Chicago was cut short by a salary dispute.

Madlock was acquired from the Texas Rangers to replace Gold Glove-winner Ron Santo at third base. To get him, the Cubs traded away future Hall-of-Fame pitcher Ferguson Jenkins.

His first season with the Cubs, Madlock's compact swing and slashing line drives became the talk of the league. In 1975, he won his first batting title with a .354 average. The next year, on the final day of the season, he edged out the Reds' Ken Griffey, Sr., to hit .339 for a second consecutive batting crown.

When it came time to negotiate his contract for the upcoming season, Madlock and his agent wanted a multi-year deal. Madlock was making $85,000 in 1976 and sought a five-year deal totaling $1.5 million, with $1 million deferred. Cubs owner Philip K. Wrigley wouldn't give. "No ballplayer is worth more than $100,00 and I'm not sure they're worth that much," he said at the time.

On January 17, 1977, Madlock was traded to the San Francisco Giants. Wrigley's public statements did nothing to encourage dejected fans: "We don't expect to win any pennants," Wrigley said. "All I'm trying to do is survive." In an ironic twist, the Cubs acquired 31-year-old outfielder Bobby Murcer in the trade and wound up giving him a five-year contract worth more money than Madlock had demanded. Murcer had one good year and was gone halfway through the 1979 season. Madlock spent two-plus seasons with the Giants before settling in Pittsburgh, where he again won batting titles in 1981 and 1983. He retired after the 1987 season with a .305 average and 2,008 career hits. Madlock later returned to the majors as a hitting coach with the Detroit Tigers.

Bobby Murcer
Outfielder, 1977-1979

Bobby Murcer was supposed to be the next Mickey Mantle when he played for the Yankees. He was a left-handed pull-hitter perfectly matched for the short-rightfield fence at Yankee Stadium. Murcer hit 139 home runs during six seasons in New York, but after he was traded to the Giants in 1975, his home run numbers dropped dramatically The swirling winds at Candlestick Park played havoc with long fly balls.

But home runs don't fully measure a hitter's worth, and Murcer was valued for his ability to get runners home. By the time he was traded to Chicago for slugger Bill Madlock, Murcer had driven in more than 90 runs five times.

In his debut season at Wrigley Field, Murcer hit 27 home runs and drove in 89 runs. But he was 31, and it was his last big year in the majors. In 1978, Murcer produced only nine home runs. In 1979, when the Cubs began dumping big salaries, Murcer was traded back to the Yankees. He spent four seasons there, mostly as a reserve. He retired in 1983. Murcer later joined the Yankees' broadcast team.

Rick "Big Daddy" Reuschel
Pitcher, 1972-1981; 1983-1984

During the 1970's, no Cubs pitcher won more games than Rick Reuschel. He led the team in wins five times and won 114 games in eight seasons.

The beefy right-hander was a constant winner when the franchise was in a state of flux. During his 10 years in Chicago, the Cubs had six managers and only one winning season. Still, Reuschel was the team's most reliable starter. Beginning in 1973, he had eight straight years of throwing at least 230 innings. His 343 starts rank him second on the Cubs' all-time list.

In 1977, Reuschel went 20-10 with a 2.79 ERA and threw four shutouts. He was selected to that year's All-Star team. In 1979, he won 18 games for the fifth-place Cubs. But early in 1981, the Cubs traded Reuschel to the Yankees, where he made a trip to the World Series. However, he missed the entire 1982 season because of a torn rotator cuff.

The Cubs re-signed Reuschel in 1983, but used him sparingly as he tried to regain his form. In 1984, when the Cubs finally were winning, injuries limited Reuschel to a 5-5 record and the highest ERA of his career. He could only sit and watch as the Cubs played post-season baseball for the first time in 40 years. The next year, Reuschel was signed by the Pirates as a free agent.

To the amazement of everyone, Reuschel went 14-8 his first year in Pittsburgh. He was named 1985 Comeback Player of the Year. In 1987, he was traded to the San Francisco Giants, where he won 36 games in two seasons and helped pitch the Giants to a division title in 1987 and the World Series in 1989. With the Giants, he was named to two more All-Star teams and twice was awarded the Gold Glove for his fielding. Reuschel retired after the 1991 season.

Bruce Sutter
Pitcher, 1976-1980

For eight years, Bruce Sutter was the most dominant relief pitcher in the National League.

The Cubs sent Sutter to the minors after signing him for $500 at age 18. In the minors, Sutter threw a blazing fastball, but blew out his elbow. Freddie Martin, the Cubs' minor-league pitching instructor, taught him to throw a new pitch, the split-fingered forkball. The move saved his career.

Used exclusively as a reliever, Sutter arrived in Chicago early in the 1976 season. He quickly became known for his calm demeanor and superb control. By season's end, he was the Cubs' closer. In 1977, he saved 31 games, the second most in the league. That year, he struck out 129 batters in 107 innings, and had an ERA of 1.34. In 1979, Sutter led the league with 37 saves and was named the Cy Young Award winner.

That offseason, Sutter became eligible for salary arbitration. He won his case and was awarded a salary of $700,000, angering Cubs owner Bill Wrigley, who'd taken over the club following his father's death. Sutter led the league with 28 saves in 1980, but when the season ended, he was traded to the St. Louis Cardinals for three players.

With the Cardinals, Sutter led the league in saves three times and in 1982, helped take St. Louis to the World Series. After four years with the Cardinals, the Atlanta Braves signed Sutter in 1985 as a free agent. The Braves gave Sutter a six-year, $10 million contract, but Sutter's favorite pitch had ruined his arm. In parts of three seasons, he recorded only 40 saves. He missed the entire 1987 season and retired after 1988. At the time he left the majors, Sutter's 300 career saves ranked him first on baseball's all-time list.

Jerry Morales
Outfielder, 1974-1977; 1981-1983

During his first two seasons in Chicago, Jerry Morales drove in 82 and 91 runs, best on the team both years. He played left field, and along with Rick Monday and Jose Cardenal, gave the last-place Cubs a superb defensive outfield.

In 1977, Morales batted .290 and was named to the All-Star team. His reward was a trade to the St. Louis Cardinals prior to the 1978 season. Morales played for three teams over the next three years before returning to the Cubs as a free agent prior to the 1981 season. Used mainly as a reserve, Morales retired after the 1983 season.

Donnie Moore
Pitcher, 1975; 1977-1979

Donnie Moore's major-league career is remembered more for the way it ended than how it began.

After pitching eight innings late in 1975, Moore joined the Cubs for good in 1977 as a reliever. For the next three years, he was closer Bruce Sutter's set-up man out of the bullpen. Moore's best year was 1978 when he won a career-high nine games for Chicago and led the team with 78 appearances. In 1980, he was traded to the St. Louis Cardinals, and three more teams over the next five years.

Moore last played for the California Angels, where in 1985, he had a 1.92 ERA and set a club record with 31 saves. A defining moment happened in 1986, when the Angels faced the Boston Red Sox for the American League championship. In Game 5, Moore was on the mound and one strike away from a trip to the World Series when Red Sox batter, outfielder Dave Henderson, hit one over the left field fence, putting the Red Sox up, 6-5. The Angels came back to tie, but in the top of the 11th inning, with Moore still on the mound, Henderson again came to the plate and hit a sacrifice fly to win the game for Boston. The Red Sox took the trip to the World Series.

Moore pitched another two seasons for California but injuries forced him to retire after the 1988 season. Ten months after leaving baseball, Moore committed suicide. He was 35.

Dave Kingman
Outfielder, 1978-1980

Dave Kingman hit home runs everywhere he went, but he so annoyed those around him that he played his career bouncing from team to team.

Kingman played for seven teams during 16 years in the majors. In 1977, he played for four teams in a single season. But desperate for offense, the Cubs signed Kingman as a free agent in 1978.

Kingman hit 28 home runs his first year in Chicago. In 1979, he did even better. He led the National League with 48 home runs and he hit a career-high .288. His 115 RBI were second only to Dave Winfield's 118. Kingman became the toast of Chicago, but the honeymoon was short-lived. Kingman was an intensely private person who preferred fishing to playing ball. He often refused to give interviews, which led to a long-running feud with the press. In 1980, Kingman injured his shoulder and missed two months. When he returned, his hitting slumped and Cubs fans began to boo him. The Cubs traded Kingman to the Mets prior to the 1981 season.

Kingman continued hitting home runs. In 1982, he again led the league with 37 home runs. After three seasons with the Mets, Kingman landed in Oakland, where he had three of his best years ever. He hit 110 home runs and drove in 303 runs in three seasons for the A's.

Kingman retired after the 1986 season when, at age 37, he was unable to find any team willing to hire a player who had hit 35 home runs the year before.

Ivan DeJesus
Shortstop, 1977-1981

Ivan DeJesus was part of two of the biggest trades in recent Cubs history. He arrived in Chicago along with Bill Buckner from the Dodgers in 1977 and stepped into the void at shortstop left by the departed Don Kessinger.

His first year with the Cubs, DeJesus helped jump-start the offense, scoring 91 runs and stealing 24 bases. In 1978, DeJesus led the league in runs scored and stole 41 bases, the most by a Cubs shortstop in 75 years. In 1980, he stole 44 bases and became the 12th player in Cubs history to hit for the cycle.

DeJesus also got rave reviews for his defense. He and second baseman Manny Trillo dazzled opponents with their acrobatic play. When Trillo was traded to the Phillies in 1979, DeJesus sulked and his play suffered. In the strike-shortened season of 1981, he batted .194. Following the season, he, too, was sent to Philadelphia in a trade that brought shortstop Larry Bowa and a rookie infielder named Ryne Sandberg to the Cubs. The trade set the stage for the Cubs' 1984 pennant run and gave Cubs fans an icon for the next 15 years.

DeJesus played three years for the Phillies and appeared in the 1983 World Series. He spent another four years with four different teams, all as a reserve, before retiring in 1988.

Bill Buckner
First baseman, 1977-1984

Bill Buckner was a fiery player who overcame a serious leg injury to win a batting title with the Cubs.

Buckner's temper was legendary while in the Dodgers' minor-league system. He destroyed water coolers, kicked batting helmets and argued with umpires. In 1975, after being called up by the Dodgers, he broke his ankle sliding into second base and missed the second half of the season. But Buckner came back to hit .301 the next year, despite playing with a leg that never properly healed. As a result, he hobbled badly the rest of his career.

When the Dodgers traded him to the Cubs prior to the 1977 season, Buckner was stunned. He popped off in the press, blasting the Cubs as losers. But gradually his aggressive style won over Cubs fans. He hated to lose and his teammates took note. Buckner became the Cubs' leader on the field. He played hard, he played hurt and he was the team's best hitter. In 1978, he led Chicago with a .323 average and in 1980, Buckner won the National League batting title with a .324 average. In spite of playing with only one good leg, Buckner twice led the league in doubles while with the Cubs.

But the constant losing ate at him. In 1980, after the Cubs finished last, Buckner ripped his teamates in the press for their uninspired play. He also continued to feud with the Cubs' front office. Early in 1984, "Billy Buc" was dealt to the Boston Red Sox for pitcher Dennis Eckersley. Buckner spent three-plus seasons in Boston and was forever immortalized for misplaying a ground ball in Game 6 of the 1986 World Series against the New York Mets. Traded to the California Angels in 1987, Buckner hung on for another three seasons before retiring in 1990. He finished with 2,715 career hits.

Jody Davis
Catcher, 1981-1988

Jody Davis was the first player the Cubs acquired when the team began its rebuilding effort in the early 1980's.

His first year in Chicago, Davis played only 56 games behind the plate because of the players' strike. The next year, the Cubs acquired catcher Keith Moreland and Davis had to hit his way back into the lineup. But in June 1982, Davis rode a 14-game hitting streak and the Cubs sent Moreland to the outfield.

Davis was a take-charge guy who didn't mind telling his pitching staff what to do. He became a leader in the clubhouse and better on offense as his playing time increased. In 1983, Davis hit 24 home runs, tops among all National League catchers and the most by a Cubs catcher since Gabby Hartnett in 1930. In 1984, he produced a career-high 94 RBI and the Cubs won the National League Eastern Division title. In the playoffs against San Diego, Davis hit two home runs and led the Cubs with six RBI. In 1986, Davis became the second Cubs catcher to win the Gold Glove Award.

But six straight years of crouching behind the plate took their toll. At 31, his batting average slipped and he was traded to the Atlanta Braves midway through the 1988 season. Davis spent two years with the Braves as a backup before retiring in 1990.

Leon "Bull" Durham
Outfielder/First baseman, 1981-1988

Power-hitter Leon Durham came to the Cubs from the St. Louis Cardinals in the trade for pitcher Bruce Sutter.

Durham started in the outfield and in 1982, batted .312 with 22 home runs and 90 RBI. He became the first Cub in 70 years to have 20 home runs and at least 20 steals in the same season. But because of injuries, the Cubs moved Durham to first base, replacing veteran Bill Buckner. Cubs fans booed and chanted, "We want Buckner!" But Durham's fiery bat soon turned the boos to cheers for "Bull!"

In 1984, Durham helped lead the Cubs to a division title. He hit 23 home runs and added 96 RBI. In the playoffs, he hit two home runs against San Diego, but his misplay of a routine ground ball in the seventh inning of Game 5 cost the Cubs the game and put the Padres in the World Series. Durham continued to provide the Cubs with power for another three-plus seasons. He had five years with 20 or more home runs and twice hit a home run in four straight games.

Early in 1988, the Cubs traded Durham to the Cincinnati Reds. He missed most of the season undergoing drug rehab and by 1989, he was out of the majors.

Keith Moreland
Outfielder, 1982-1987

Bobby Keith Moreland was a tough Texan whose booming bat kept him in the majors for 11 full seasons.

Moreland started as an all-American third baseman at the University of Texas, but he also played varsity football. His hard-nosed approach earned him two things: a reputation as a hot-head and a nickname, "Zonk." Moreland was converted to a catcher by his first major league team, the Phillies. But when he arrived in Chicago in 1982, competition for the catcher's job landed him in the outfield.

For the next six years, Moreland's dependable bat made him a major cog in the Cubs' offense. He twice hit over .300 and actually seemed to hit better with men on base. In 1985, Moreland had his best season ever, driving in 106 runs and putting together an 18-game hitting streak. He had three seasons with 30 doubles and in 1986, led the team with 79 RBI. The following year, he hit a career-high 27 home runs.

Desperate for pitching help prior to the 1988 season, the Cubs traded Moreland to San Diego for reliever Goose Gossage. Moreland played in the American League for a year before retiring after the 1989 season.

Larry Bowa
Shortstop, 1982-1985

Shortstop Larry Bowa had a strong arm, fast legs and a glove like a magnet.

He came to the Cubs in 1982 after 11 great years with the Philadelphia Phillies, where he won two Gold Gloves, one World Series ring and five All-Star appearances.

Bowa was known for his quickness. He had nine years with at least 20 stolen bases and in 1972, he led the league with 13 triples. But it was his glove that kept him in the lineup. Bowa led the league's shortstops in fielding six times.

Bowa came to the Cubs at age 36 in the same trade that brought Ryne Sandberg to Chicago. Bowa's experience on winning teams was just what Chicago needed and his aggressive style of play helped fire up the Cubs. He treated the opposing team like the enemy and played accordingly. In 1983, Bowa was named team captain. But his weak hitting led to frequent benchings and 1984 was his last season as an everyday player. Bowa was traded to the Mets during the 1985 season and retired that fall.

In 1987, he was named manager of the San Diego Padres, but his temper wore thin and he was fired early in 1988. In 2001, he returned as manager of the Philadelphia Phillies.

Ryne Sandberg
Second baseman, 1982-1994; 1996-1997

For the better part of two decades, Ryne Sandberg was the Cubs' best and most popular player.

After arriving from the Phillies in 1982, Sandberg started at third base and had an immediate impact on offense. He stole 32 bases his first year, the first of five straight years with at least 30 steals. He also set the Cubs' record for runs scored by a rookie, with 103, best on the team that year. In 1983, the Cubs moved Sandberg to second base were he proved to be a natural. He led the league's second basemen in fielding and won his first Gold Glove award.

When the Cubs won a division title in 1984, it was "Ryno" who led the way. He led Cubs hitters with a .314 average and led the league in runs scored. In the middle of a tight pennant race, he twice hit home runs off Cardinals reliever Bruce Sutter on June 23 to rally the Cubs to an extra-inning win. His seven RBI and late inning heroics seemed to signal that it was finally the Cubs' year. For his efforts that season, Sandberg was chosen the National League's most valuable player.

Over the next decade, Sandberg continued to set new marks for a second baseman and became the standard against which others were measured. Starting in 1984, Sandberg was named to 10 consecutive All-Star teams and won nine Gold Glove awards. In 1989, he set a major-league record for second basemen by playing 90 straight games without committing an error. When the Cubs again won a division title in 1989, Sandberg batted .400 in the postseason series against the San Francisco Giants. In 1990 he had his best year yet.

Lee Smith
Pitcher, 1980-1987

At six-foot-six and 225 pounds, Lee Arthur Smith was one of baseball's most menacing figures on the mound. Yet there was no mystery about him. When Smith entered the game, he brought the heat. The only mystery was whether opposing batters could handle it.

The Cubs drafted Smith in the second round of the 1975 draft, but his impact wasn't felt until 1982. Smith retired 19 straight batters late that season and the Cubs knew they finally had found a successor to closer Bruce Sutter. The next year, Smith had a 1.65 ERA, racked up 29 saves and was named to the All-Star team. Between 1984 and 1987, he was money in the bank. He had at least 30 saves each of those four years, becoming the first National League reliever to achieve this feat.

Then, suddenly, the Cubs traded Smith to the Boston Red Sox, a huge mistake. Smith was at his peak and over the next eight years, piled up 291 saves. He had six straight seasons with at least 30 saves and led the league in saves in 1991 and 1992, pitching for the St. Louis Cardinals. By the time he retired after the 1997 season, Smith had 478 career saves, ranking him number one on baseball's all-time list. His 180 saves for the Cubs remains the team's record.

Dallas Green
Executive, 1981-1987

Dallas Green was a career baseball man who put together the first Cubs team to win a title in 40 years.

When the Cubs tapped Green, he was managing the Phillies, having played and coached his way through the team's system since 1967. In 1980, his first year as Phillies manager, Green won the World Series.

When the Tribune Company bought the Cubs from the Wrigley family in 1981, the new owners wanted a fresh start and they recruited Green to be general manager. Almost immediately, Green, a keen judge of talent, began to overhaul the Cubs' roster. He plucked Keith Moreland and Ryne Sandberg from the Phillies' system. He traded for Leon Durham and drafted Jody Davis from the Cardinals' minor-league system. In 1984, he stole Ron Cey from the Dodgers and Gary Matthews and Bob Dernier from the Phillies. He also brought in Jim Frey as manager and when the Cubs needed another arm for their 1984 pennant drive, he got Rick Sutcliffe from Cleveland. The mix of veterans and rookies gelled perfectly to give Cubs fans a summer to remember.

However, Green's abrasive style clashed with Tribune management and he was gone after the 1987 season. But his ability to judge talent paid dividends for years to come. Green was responsible for drafting such future stars as Shawon Dunston, Rafael Palmeiro and Greg Maddux. The team that won the 1989 National League Eastern Division title was largely his creation.

In 1993, Green returned to the dugout to manage the New York Mets for four seasons. He later worked as a scout.

Ron Cey
Third baseman, 1983-1986

Slugger Ron Cey arrived in Chicago in time to help the Cubs win their first title in 40 years.

Cey was a six-time All-Star from the Dodgers whose booming bat gave the Cubs' offense a much-needed jolt. The Cubs hadn't had a home-run threat at third like Cey, who had hit 228 home runs in Los Angeles, since the days of Ron Santo. Cey continued the pace in Chicago. The "friendly confines" were just that for Cey. In 1983, he collected 24 home runs and 90 RBI.

Cey was never a superb fielder and his batting average never exceeded .290 in any of his 17 years in the majors. But he could be counted on to produce runs in key situations. With a short stocky build that earned him the nickname "the Penguin," Cey battled through injuries to lead the Cubs in home runs and RBI in 1984 when the team made the playoffs. By 1985, Cey was 38 and his range at third had diminished. He hit 22 home runs in his last season as an everyday player. Cey was traded to the Oakland A's after the 1986 season and retired the next year.

Mel Hall
Outfielder, 1981-1984

Mel Hall hit a home run in his first major-league game, but he didn't become a regular with the Cubs until two years later. When he finally was allowed to play every day, the speedy outfielder had a tremendous year. Despite missing two months with injuries in 1983, Hall batted .283 with 17 home runs and 56 RBI to finish third in the Rookie of the Year balloting. During one stretch in late August, Hall hit five home runs in 11 at bats. Experts around the National League predicted super-stardom for Hall.

But in the middle of the 1984 season, with the Cubs atop the standings, Hall was dealt to the Cleveland Indians along with Joe Carter for pitcher Rick Sutcliffe. The move put the Cubs in the playoffs as Sutcliffe won 16 straight games.

Hall never became the slugger everyone expected. In early 1985, he was injured in an auto accident and missed almost the entire season. Over the next four years with the Indians, Hall twice hit 18 home runs, but was traded to the Yankees in 1989. His 19 home runs and 80 RBI in 1991 would be the high points of his career. Hall retired after the 1992 season and later played in Japan, before attempting a brief comeback with Giants in 1996.

Joe Carter
Outfielder, 1984

Outfielder Joe Carter was so highly regarded that the Cubs made him the second overall pick of the 1981 draft. But Carter played only 23 games for the Cubs before being dealt to Cleveland for pitcher Rick Sutcliffe.

Over the next 15 years, Carter became one of the majors' most consistent run producers. Despite playing for some lousy teams, Carter had 10 seasons with more than 100 RBI. During his career, he hit 396 home runs. Carter was that rare combination of power and speed, stealing more than 20 bases six times. He will be forever remembered for his game-winning home run in Game 6 of the 1993 World Series for the Toronto Blue Jays.

In 2001, he returned to Chicago, replacing Steve Stone as color commentator in the Channel 9 broadcast booth.

Jim Frey
Manager, 1984-1986

Jim Frey spent four decades in professional baseball as a player, coach and manager. He spent the first 14 years as a minor league player winning two batting titles, but never played a day in the majors. For another 15 years, he coached and managed in the Baltimore Orioles' minor-league system.

In 1980, Frey was tapped to manage the Kansas City Royals and in his first season, he took the team to the World Series. But the team lost in six games to the Philadelphia Phillies, managed by Dallas Green.

The next year, Green was in Chicago as Cubs general manager and by 1984, he was looking for a new skipper. Green tapped Frey, believing his winning record and no-nonsense approach were just what the Cubs needed. Together, they set about revamping the Cubs' lineup. Green made trades for proven veterans like Gary Matthews, Bob Dernier and Rick Sutcliffe, and Frey soon had the Cubs on the way to their first title in 39 years. For his efforts, Frey was named National League Manager of the Year.

But Frey's magic seemed to last only one year. In 1985, the Cubs reverted to their losing ways and finished fourth. When the team got off to a 23-33 start in 1986, Frey was replaced by Gene Michael in June.

Dennis Eckersley
Pitcher, 1984-1986

Unfortunately for Cubs fans, Dennis Eckersley's best seasons happened before and after he played for the Cubs.

Eckersley won 20 games with the Boston Red Sox in 1978 and threw a no-hitter for Cleveland in 1979. But the pressure to win and a failed marriage caused him to start drinking heavily, and by the time he arrived in Chicago, he'd lost his edge.

The Cubs acquired Eckersley in the middle of the 1984 season and put him into the starting rotation. But the team gave him little run support. In three seasons, Eckersley won 27 games. Four days before the start of the 1987 season, Eckersley was traded to the Oakland A's. Finally sober, he was put in the bullpen, where he emerged as one of baseball's most dominant closers. Eckersley twice led the American League in saves and his ability to close out games took Oakland to three straight World Series. In 10-plus seasons, Eckersley recorded 390 saves, the third best of all-time. He retired after the 1998 season.

Steve Trout
Pitcher, 1983-1987

Steve Trout was an erratic left-hander whose only big year coincided with the Cubs' 1984 division title.

Trout grew up the son of a famous baseball father, Dizzy Trout, a pitcher for the Detroit Tigers who twice won 20 games in the 1940's. Dizzy died when Steve was 14, leaving a son determined to follow in his father's footsteps. In 1976, Steve made it to the big leagues when the White Sox chose him with their first-round draft pick.

The results were disappointing. In five seasons on the South Side, Trout gained a reputation as a flake. Only once did he win more than nine games for the White Sox. His career record stood at 37-40 when he was traded to the Cubs in 1983.

His first year with the Cubs, Trout went 10-14 and didn't impress anyone. But before the 1984 season began, Cubs pitching coach Billy Connors convinced Trout to take his game seriously. Trout hit the gym and changed his diet to restore his fading career. That year, he went 13-7 and led the Cubs' pitching staff in innings and starts. He threw two shutouts and had a string of six straight wins. In Game 2 of the National League pennant series against San Diego, Trout held the Padres to five hits and the Cubs won, 4-2.

Following the season, Trout was a free agent. He signed a five-year contract with the Cubs for a reported $4.5 million, but he reverted to form and went 20-17 over the next three seasons. Trout was traded to the New York Yankees late in 1987 and retired in 1989 after two final seasons in Seattle.

Gary Matthews
Outfielder, 1984-1987

Gary Matthews, 1973 Rookie of the Year with the San Francisco Giants, knew only one way to play the game — all out. In Chicago 11 years later, he stayed true to form. He dove for balls, stormed the outfield wall and delivered key runs when the Cubs needed them most. Pete Rose, a former teammate in Philadelphia, nicknamed him "Sarge" because of his take-charge, all-out attitude.

Matthews came to Chicago from the Phillies, where he had won a World Series in 1980 under manager Dallas Green, now general manager of the Cubs. Matthews, 34, provided immediate help in the outfield and at the plate. He and teammates Bobby Dernier and Keith Moreland gave the Cubs three former Phillies in the outfield and a new fiery attitude in the clubhouse.

In 1984, Matthews led the league in walks, on-base percentage and game-winning RBI. In the NLCS against San Diego, he produced two home runs and five runs batted in. But injuries forced him to miss half of the 1985 season. In 1986, he came back to hit 21 home runs, but it was his last season as a regular. He was released by the Cubs in 1985 and finished the season with the Seattle Mariners before retiring.

He later helped broadcast games for the Toronto Blue Jays. In 2001, his son, Gary Matthews, Jr., took over as the Cubs' everyday centerfielder.

Bobby Dernier
Outfielder, 1984-1987

Speedy outfielder Bobby Dernier came to the Cubs in the same trade that brought Gary Matthews from Philadelphia. Dernier soon replaced Mel Hall as the Cubs' everyday centerfielder.

Dernier ran down almost everything in sight. He also ran wild on the basepaths. In 1984, he stole 45 bases, the most by a Cub since Johnny Evers stole 46 in 1907. At the top of the batting order, Dernier and second baseman Ryne Sandberg became known as the "Daily Double" for their ability to get on base in front of the Cubs' sluggers.

Dernier's speed allowed him to cover a lot of ground and his dazzling defensive work in 1984 made him the first Cubs outfielder to ever win a Gold Glove award. But injuries slowed him the next two seasons and his batting average dropped. By 1987, Dernier was no longer playing every day. He batted .317 and hit a career-high eight home runs, but stole only 16 bases. Dernier signed with the Phillies as a free agent and played two more years as a reserve before retiring following the 1989 season.

Scott Sanderson
Pitcher, 1984-1989

Scott Sanderson spent parts of 19 seasons in the majors, but his six years with the Cubs were marked more by injuries than by victories.

Before he joined the Cubs in 1984, Sanderson had won 56 games in six years with the Montreal Expos, a control pitcher who rarely walked opposing batters. Sanderson won four of his first five starts in Chicago, but back spasms sidelined him for several months and limited him to only eight wins. In 1985, torn knee ligaments ended his season in August. The next year, he won nine games and threw the lone shutout of his Cubs career, but injuries interrupted again. He missed almost the entire 1988 season due to back surgery. He returned in 1989 to have his best year as a Cub, winning 11 games. But it was also his last season in Chicago as Sanderson filed for free agency and signed with Oakland in 1990. Finally healthy, he won a career-high 17 games.

Over the next six years, Sanderson pitched for five different teams before retiring in 1996.

Rick Sutcliffe
Pitcher, 1984-1991

Rick Sutcliffe's arrival in June 1984 helped secure the Cubs' first title in 40 years.

Sutcliffe was a star at a young age. His first year with the Dodgers, he won 17 games and was named the 1979 National League Rookie of the Year. In Cleveland in 1982, he was the ace of the Indians' staff. Set to become a free agent after the 1984 season, Sutcliffe was traded to the Cubs for Joe Carter and Mel Hall, a deal that benefitted both clubs. Carter became a star in Cleveland and Sutcliffe helped deliver a pennant to Chicago.

Sutcliffe was overpowering, going 16-1 and leading the Cubs to the postseason. He won 14 straight at season's end and was named the league's Cy Young Award winner. The Cubs re-signed him to a five-year $9.5 million contract, then the richest in club history. But 1985 found Sutcliffe sidelined with injuries and an 8-8 record. In 1986, he went 5-14, largely because he was given the lowest run support of any NL starter.

Sutcliffe returned to form in 1987, when he led the league with 18 wins despite pitching for a last-place team. Sutcliffe became the workhorse of the Cubs' pitching staff, throwing more than 225 innings for three straight seasons. When the Cubs repeated as Eastern Division champs in 1989, Sutcliffe contributed 16 victories.

But shoulder problems limited him to only five starts in 1990 and six wins in 1991. His contract with the Cubs over, Sutcliffe signed with the Baltimore Orioles as a free agent in 1992. There, he won 36 games in two years before finishing up with St. Louis for one final season in 1994. He later worked as a broadcaster for the San Diego Padres.

Leon Durham and Jody Davis
Wrigley Field, 1984

The combination of Leon Durham and Jody Davis provided a dazzling spark for the Cubs' division-winning season of 1984. The duo ranked second and third on the team in RBI, Durham with 96 and Davis with 94, the most by a Cubs' catcher since Gabby Hartnett in 1930. Both players provided leadership in the clubhouse and on the field. In the five-game series against the Padres for the National League championship, both players hit two home runs.

Rafael Palmeiro
Outfielder, 1986-1988

Rafael Palmeiro is another one that got away from the Chicago Cubs.

A three-time All-American at Mississippi State, Palmeiro was the Cubs' first-round draft pick in 1985. A year later, at age 21, he was in the majors. In 1987, he hit 14 home runs for the Cubs, despite playing half the season in the minors. Splitting time between the outfield and first base, Palmeiro hit 41 doubles and batted .307 as an everyday player in 1988.

But after four losing seasons, the Cubs' front office was desperate to put together a winning team, which meant replacing closer Lee Smith. And so after the 1988 season, Chicago traded Palmeiro to the Texas Rangers in a nine-player deal that brought reliever Mitch Williams to the Cubs. To make matters worse, the Cubs threw in pitcher Jamie Moyer, who eventually developed into a winner in Seattle. Williams would be gone from Chicago after two seasons and out of baseball by 1995. Palmeiro would go on to become one of the American League's most lethal power hitters. At the start of the 2001 season, Palmeiro had 400 career home runs and seven seasons with more than 100 runs batted in.

Andre Dawson
Outfielder, 1987-1992

After 10 seasons with the Montreal Expos, outfielder Andre Dawson, 32, was a free agent. His chronically bad knees ached after a decade on artificial turf and he wanted a change of scenery, so Dawson offered the Cubs a blank check, literally. He told general manager Dallas Green to simply fill in the salary amount for the 1987 season. The Cubs offered $500,000, a steal since Dawson went on to put up the best numbers of his career. "The Hawk," as he was known, hit 49 home runs and drove in 137 runs to lead the league in both categories. He was named the league's most valuable player. It was the first time that a player from a last-place team received the award.

Over the next five seasons, Dawson continued to lead the offensive charge for the Cubs. He had three seasons with more than 100 runs batted in, and also led the Cubs in home runs three times. In 1988, he was selected to the first of five consecutive All-Star teams. That year, he also won his eighth Gold Glove award.

Following the 1992 season, Dawson, again a free agent, signed with the Red Sox. His bad knees didn't allow him to play the outfield any longer and he became Boston's designated hitter for two seasons. In 1995, he returned to his native Miami with the expansion Florida Marlins. No longer an everyday player, Dawson retired after the 1996 season with 438 home runs and 2,774 hits.

Don Zimmer
Manager, 1988-1991

Don Zimmer is a career baseball man who has spent more than 50 years in the game.

As a player, Zimmer spent parts of 12 seasons in the majors, mostly on the bench. His fame came as a major-league manager, piloting the Padres, Red Sox and Rangers, before being named manager of the Cubs in 1988.

Saddled with a team that had finished last in 1987, Zimmer and general manager Jim Frey set about re-making the Cubs' roster. By Opening Day 1989, they had overhauled the catching staff, strengthened the bullpen and promoted several minor-league prospects, including outfielder Jerome Walton. That year, Zimmer got career years out of Ryne Sandberg and Greg Maddux. The result was 93 wins and the Eastern Division title. Zimmer was named the National League Manager of the Year. However, the season ended on a down note when the Cubs lost to the San Francisco Giants in a five-game NLCS.

In 1990, the Cubs reverted to form and finished fourth. When the team struggled again in 1991, Zimmer was replaced midway through the year. He spent four seasons as a coach with the Red Sox and Rockies before joining the New York Yankees as a bench coach in 1996.

Greg Maddux
Pitcher, 1986-1992

Greg Maddux is proof positive that pitching is more than the ability to throw hard.

Maddux was the Cubs' second-round pick in the 1984 draft who arrived in the majors two years later. Only 20, he struggled against big-league hitters. In 1987, he went 6-14 and had an ERA of 5.61. But the young rookie learned something while sitting on the bench between starts. A Cubs teammate recalled, "He'd always be in the dugout watching players on the other team, studying the hitters and trying to learn a thing or two that he could use the next time he faced them."

Maddux proved a quick study. In 1988, he won 18 games for the fourth-place Cubs, including a streak of 26 scoreless innings. When the Cubs won the 1989 Eastern Division title, Maddux led the staff with 19 victories. He became the Cubs' most reliable starter, leading the league in starts for the next two seasons and winning 15 games each year. He also became a superb fielder, winning three straight Gold Glove awards. In 1992, Maddux went 20-11, threw four shutouts and led the league in innings pitched. He was chosen the NL's Cy Young award winner.

Maddux became a free agent at the end of the season and wound up signing with the Atlanta Braves, who had just won back-to-back NL titles. The loss was devastating for the Cubs as Maddux quickly became the league's most dominant pitcher. He won 20 games in 1993 for the Braves and went on to win three consecutive Cy Young awards. In addition, Maddux won the ERA crown in four of his first six years with the Braves. By the start of the 2001 season, Maddux had won 240 games in the majors, 145 of them after leaving the Cubs.

Shawon Dunston
Shortstop, 1985-1995; 1997

The Cubs made Shawon Dunston the first player chosen in the 1982 draft.

By Opening Day 1985, Dunston was the Cubs' starting shortstop. He had an exceptionally strong arm, even for a shortstop, but his hitting was weak and his fielding erratic and after only half a season, he was shipped back to the minors. Dunston returned to the majors the next year, in a big way. He hit 17 home runs and drove in 68 runs, the most by a Cubs' shortstop in 25 years. In 1988, Dunston led the Cubs with 30 stolen bases and was named to the All-Star team.

Dunston showed exceptional range in the field, leading NL shortstops in put-outs three times. At the plate, he became one of the league's toughest men to walk. A herniated disc and subsequent back surgery caused him to miss almost all of 1992 and 1993, but when Dunston was finally healthy, he had a career year in 1995, batting .296 and driving in 69 runs.

In 1996, Dunston signed as a free agent with the San Francisco Giants, where he spent one year before returning briefly to the Cubs in 1997. Sold to the Pittsburgh Pirates that same season, Dunston became a baseball gypsy, playing for three teams in two years. Late in 1998, he was back with the Giants who converted him to an outfielder.

Mitch Williams
Pitcher, 1989-1990

Mitch Williams was an explosive presence on the mound who did everything possible to earn his nickname, "Wild Thing."

Williams arrived in Chicago in 1989 from the Texas Rangers, where he worked 231 games in three seasons as a reliever. In his first outing for the Cubs, on Opening Day at Wrigley Field, Williams entered the game against the Phillies to protect a 5-4 lead. He walked the bases loaded, then struck out three straight batters to preserve the win. Williams provided high drama that ensured no one ever left a Cubs game early.

Williams never tired of taking the ball in key situations. In 1989, he led all NL pitchers with 76 appearances and notched 36 saves for the Cubs. But in 1990, he was less effective. He spent a month on the disabled list with a knee injury and earned only 16 saves. His strikeouts dropped and his walks rose. Two days into the 1991 season, the Cubs sent Williams to the Philadelphia Phillies for two minor-league relievers. It was another trade that backfired for Chicago.

Williams rebounded to save 102 games for the Phillies over the next three seasons. But it was Joe Carter's game-winning home run for Toronto in Game 6 of the 1993 World Series for which Williams will, unfortunately, be long remembered.

Damon Berryhill
Catcher, 1987-1991

Doug Dascenzo
Outfielder, 1988-1992

Catcher Damon Berryhill was a first-round draft pick whose career with the Cubs was regularly interrupted by injuries.

In parts of five seasons with Chicago, Berryhill caught more than 65 games only twice. In 1988, he replaced veteran catcher Jody Davis behind the plate and gained a reputation for throwing out opposing basestealers. But shoulder surgery cost him half of 1989 and most of the 1990 season. His batting average plummeted and he was traded to the Atlanta Braves late in 1991.

With Atlanta, Berryhill was the everyday catcher for two seasons. But his weak bat got him traded to the Boston Red Sox in 1994. Berryhill spent three of the next four seasons as a backup with three different teams before retiring after the 1997 season.

Doug Dascenzo was a speedy outfielder whose career with the Cubs contained some notable firsts.

Called up from the minors late in 1988, Dascenzo became the first Cubs player to get three hits in his first major-league game. In 1991, he appeared as a relief pitcher in three games, the only Cubs position player to do so in the 20th century. That same season, he finished a string of 242 consecutive games without an error, the longest streak by an outfielder to start his career in major league history.

But Dascenzo's lack of power brought an end to his time with the Cubs. In three seasons as an everyday player, he hit only two home runs and drove in 64 runs. He was released after the 1992 season and played with the Texas Rangers in 1993. In 1996, he appeared briefly with the San Diego Padres.

Luis Salazar
Infielder, 1989-1992

Veteran Luis Salazar came to Chicago late in the 1989 season as the Cubs chased their first division title in five years. Salazar paid immediate dividends, hitting .325 in the season's final five weeks.

On September 9, Salazar single-handedly won a key game for Chicago. The Cardinals were at Wrigley Field, locked in a tight race with the Cubs. In the eighth inning, Salazar hit a single and tied the game, 2-2. In the 10th, his RBI double won it. The Cubs opened up a game-and-a-half lead over the Cardinals and never looked back. In the NL championship series against the Giants, Salazar batted .368.

Salazar alternated playing time between third base and the outfield over the next three seasons. In 1991, he hit a career-high 14 home runs. Salazar retired after the 1992 season.

Paul Assenmacher
Pitcher, 1989-1993

Left-handed pitcher Paul Assenmacher was the workhorse of the Cubs' bullpen for four seasons.

Acquired from the Atlanta Braves late in 1989, Assenmacher's ability to pitch every other day made him manager Don Zimmer's secret weapon. For the next three years, he appeared in at least 70 games, the first Cubs reliever ever to do so.

Assenmacher was traded to the Yankees in August 1993 for outfielder Karl Rhodes. It was a huge loss for the Cubs. Rhodes hit 28 home runs in less than 18 months, then was traded to Boston in 1995 and out of the majors the next year. Assenmacher landed in Cleveland in 1995 and for the next five years, anchored the Indians' bullpen, helping pitch Cleveland to two World Series.

Jerome Walton
Outfielder, 1989-1992

Jerome Walton was a speedy outfielder whose best season was his first.

In 1989, Walton took the National League by storm, batting .293 and stealing 24 bases. He highlighted the year with a 30-game hitting streak, the longest by a Cub in the 20th century and second-longest by a rookie in major-league history. Walton's speed allowed him to cover a lot of ground as a centerfielder for the Cubs and when Chicago faced the Giants in the 1989 playoffs, he batted .364. All this got Walton named the NL Rookie of the Year.

In 1990, a broken left hand limited Walton to 101 games and his average dropped to .263. The next year it dropped to .219 and Walton was benched for the last month of the season. In 1992, he played only 30 games for Chicago and was released after the season. Walton bounced back and forth between the major and minor leagues for parts of six years with five different teams. He was never an everyday player again.

Ryne Sandberg
Wrigley Field, 1990

In 1990, Ryne Sandberg had one of the best seasons ever for a second baseman.

He led the league with 40 home runs, the first time a second baseman led the league since Rogers Hornsby in 1925. It also made him the first second baseman to hit more than 30 home runs for two consecutive years. In addition, Sandberg led the league in total bases and runs scored. And he hit .306 while driving in 100 runs, the second highest by a Cubs second baseman.

In the field, Sandberg also set new marks in 1990. By June, he had completed a streak of 123 errorless games, a record for a second baseman. He also won his eighth consecutive Gold Glove award, the first second baseman to win that many in a row.

Sandberg played at his peak for another four seasons, but at age 34, he suddenly retired in the middle of 1994. After a slow start, Sandberg shocked Cubs fans by leaving the game on June 13. But the next fall, having put his personal life in order, he announced his return. His bat hadn't missed a beat. Sandberg belted 25 home runs and drove in 92 runs in 1996. But 1997 was to be his final year. At age 38, Sandberg retired for good with 2,386 career hits and a .285 batting average. He ranks among the Cubs' top five career leaders in almost every offensive category.

Mark Grace
First baseman, 1988-2000

Mark Grace is living proof that scouting amateur ballplayers is an inexact science.

The Cubs picked Grace in the 24th round of the 1985 draft and from there, he took off. His first year in the minors, Grace won a batting title. The next year, he drove in 101 runs and was named the Eastern League's most valuable player. In 1988, the Cubs called him up and Grace was named Rookie of the Year by *The Sporting News*. In 1989, his .314 batting average was fourth best in the league. In the playoffs against San Francisco, Grace went 11 for 17 and drove in eight runs in the five-game series.

Grace also developed into one of the best defensive players in the majors. Starting in 1991, he led first basemen in putouts for three straight years. His graceful glovework became the standard by which other first basemen were judged. Along the way, he won four Gold Glove awards and was selected to three All-Star teams.

At the plate, Grace also excelled. In 1995, his 51 doubles led the league. He had a keen batting eye and was regularly ranked one of the five toughest players to strike out. During the Cubs' eight losing seasons in the 1990's, Grace was often the best reason to visit the ballpark.

Sammy Sosa
Outfielder, 1992 -

The Texas Rangers signed Sammy Sosa out of the Dominican Republic at age 16 and Sosa did little to attract attention initially. His first seven seasons, he never hit more than 15 home runs in any year. In March 1992, the Cubs acquired Sosa from the White Sox, but he played only 57 games his first year because of injuries.

But in 1993, at 24, Sosa broke out. He hit 33 home runs and stole 36 bases, becoming the Cubs' first 30-30 man. He also set a team record with nine consecutive hits. By 1995, his 36 home runs and 119 RBI were second-best in the league and he was named to his first All-Star team. In 1996, Sosa missed the last six weeks of the season with a broken hand, yet still hit 40 home runs and drove in 100 runs.

By now, age and the gym had bulked up Sosa's once-thin 185-pound frame and his power numbers exploded. But along with the home runs came a growing number of strike-outs. In 1997, Sosa led the league with 174 wiffs. His walk totals increased, too, as opposing pitchers began choosing to pitch around him. Despite hitting in a weak lineup that gave him little protection, Sosa became a more selective hitter and in 1998, he gave Cubs fans a season to remember.

Joe Girardi
Catcher, 1989-1992; 2000 -

Given his finesse with a pitching staff, it should be no surprise that Joe Girardi has played in six postseasons with three teams. Girardi's leadership behind the plate has made him a sought-after commodity in the majors.

Girardi made it to Chicago in 1989, sharing time behind the plate with Damon Berryhill. The next year, he became the Cubs' everyday catcher. But Girardi missed most of 1991 because of hand surgery. The next year, he played with a bad back but still managed to hit .270.

Girardi was chosen by the Colorado Rockies in the 1993 expansion draft and spent three seasons there. Following the 1995 season, he was traded to the New York Yankees, where he helped the team to three World Series in four years. In New York, he was also behind the plate for two no-hitters, one of them a perfect game. Girardi rejoined the Cubs as a free agent in 2000 and made the All-Star team.

Harry Caray
Broadcaster, 1982-1997

For the better part of two decades, this is how most Cubs fans saw announcer Harry Caray. High above the Wrigley Field grandstand, his rendition of "Take Me Out to the Ballgame" during the seventh-inning stretch became one of baseball's most endearing traditions. His colorful personality and signature phrase, "Holy Cow!" gained the team a legion of fans nationwide. Through the lean years, Harry Caray came to embody the eternal optimism of Cubs fans everywhere.

Caray spent 35 years behind the mike for three other teams before joining the Cubs in 1982. Unlike most modern announcers, Caray never made a secret of who he was rooting for and in 1989, he was honored with the Ford C. Frick award at the Baseball Hall of Fame for his five decades behind the mike.

Caray died during spring training in Arizona in 1998. In Chicago, his funeral was carried live by radio and WGN-TV as thousands lined the sidewalks outside Holy Name Cathedral to honor his passing.

Steve Stone
Broadcaster, 1983-2000

Former pitcher Steve Stone joined Harry Caray in the Cubs' broadcast booth in 1983 and for the next 15 years, the duo became synonymous with Cubs baseball.

As color man, Stone would discuss the finer points of the game while Caray called the play-by-play, often with humorous results. Caray was likely to say anything and Stone played his straight man. They would name-drop about visiting dignitaries or wish a Cubs fan "happy birthday," often leaving it up to the television viewer to follow the action on the field. Through it all, Stone and Caray became inseparable in the hearts and minds of Cubs fans. When Stone wrote a book about his career, he entitled it, "Where's Harry?" Stone retired after the 2000 season and returned to Arizona to oversee his thriving restaurant business.

Randy Myers
Pitcher, 1993-1995

Pitcher Randy Myers became one of the Cubs' most dependable closers during his three years in Chicago.

Myers came to Chicago as a free agent in 1993 after spending time in New York and Cincinnati. His first year with the Cubs, Myers led the league with a club-record 53 saves. He proved to be money in the bank for Chicago as he saved all but four of 57 chances. This for a team that won 84 games and finished fourth.

The players' strike limited Myers to only 21 saves in 1994, but the next year, he came back to save 38 games, the best record in the league. And he was named to his second straight All-Star team.

In his three years in Chicago, Myers saved 112 games. But following the 1995 season, the Cubs let him go to Baltimore as a free agent. In 1997, with the Orioles, Myers led the American League with 45 saves. He split 1998 with Toronto and San Diego before retiring with 347 career saves.

Steve Buechele
Third baseman, 1992-1995

Steve Buechele spent seven years in the majors before joining the Cubs in 1992.

Buechele began his baseball career at Stanford, where he roomed with John Elway. The Texas Rangers drafted him out of college and in 1985, he made it to the majors with Texas. Buechele became known as an excellent defensive third baseman but only an average hitter. He played for Texas, then Pittsburgh, before being traded to the Cubs.

Buechele's best season in Chicago was his first. In 1993, he batted .272 with 15 home runs and 65 runs batted in. In the field, he led the league's third basemen in fielding percentage, committing only eight errors all season. But his numbers slipped in 1995 and after a slow start in 1996, the Cubs released him. Buechele played a final nine games with Texas before retiring.

Mike Morgan
Pitcher, 1992-1995; 1998

Mike Morgan is one of the most-traveled pitchers in baseball history. When he signed with the Cubs in 1992, it was his seventh big-league club.

Morgan's first season in Chicago was outstanding. He went 16-8, won seven straight games midseason and threw a career-high 240 innings. But on Opening Day 1993, Morgan lost 1-0 to Atlanta. It would begin a pattern of Morgan getting almost no run support from his Cubs teammates. He ended the season with a 10-15 record, with the Cubs scoring only 26 runs in his 15 losses. Injuries limited Morgan to 15 starts in 1994 and a dismal 2-10 record.

After only four starts in 1995, Morgan was traded to the Cardinals. He pitched for six different teams over the next five years, including a brief return to the Cubs in 1998. In 1999, at age 39, he won 13 games for Texas, before pitching for Arizona in 2000.

Rey Sanchez
Infielder, 1991-1997

Rey Sanchez was a slick-fielding infielder whose time in Chicago was marred by time on the disabled list.

In only two of six seasons did Sanchez play in more than 100 games a year. Originally a shortstop, he moved to second base after the retirement of Ryne Sandberg in June 1994. Sanchez hit .285 that year, but the next year, hand and wrist injuries held him back. In 1996, Sanchez played in 95 games and hit just .211. The next August, he was traded to the New York Yankees for a minor-league pitching prospect. Sanchez continued playing for the Giants and Royals.

Glenallen Hill
Outfielder, 1993-1994; 1998-2000

Something about playing for the Cubs seemed to agree with Glenallen Hill, who played some of his best baseball during two stints with Chicago.

Hill came to the Cubs from Cleveland in the middle of 1993 and batted .345, with 10 home runs in only 31 games. But as the Cubs' fourth outfielder, he saw limited action in 1994 and so in 1995, as a free agent, he signed with the Giants. After three years in San Francisco, Hill rejoined the Cubs midway through 1998 and batted .351 over the second half of the year.

In 1999, Hill batted .300 with 20 home runs and 55 RBI, despite playing in only 99 games. That year, he established the Cubs' single-season record with four pinch-hit home runs. In July 2000, Hill was traded to the Yankees for two minor-league pitchers.

Steve Trachsel
Pitcher, 1993-1999

Steve Trachsel never tired of taking the mound for the Cubs. Starting in 1996, he pitched more than 200 innings four straight years. The results were mixed. Trachsel rarely walked batters, but he gave up home runs in droves. He led the league in long balls allowed in 1997.

His first full year in Chicago, Trachsel was named *The Sporting News'* 1994 Rookie Pitcher of the Year. Curiously enough, his success happened away from Wrigley Field. Trachsel was a perfect 8-0 on the road. At home, he went 1-7.

Trachsel endured a 7-13 season in 1995, but came back the next year to go 13-9 and make the All-Star team. His best year with the Cubs came in 1998, when he went 15-8. In a one-game playoff against the Giants, he threw five no-hit innings and helped propel the Cubs into the playoffs. But 1999 was a bust. Trachsel lost 18 games. He signed with Tampa Bay as a free agent for 2000, but his 8-15 record soon got him traded to the New York Mets, where he continued to struggle.

Jim Riggleman
Manager, 1995-1999

Jim Riggleman led the Cubs to the postseason his fourth year as manager.

Riggleman never played in the majors, but coached and managed in the minors for a decade. In late 1992, he made the majors as manager of the struggling San Diego Padres, but was fired after the Padres finished fourth in the strike-shortened season of 1994. Not long afterwards, newly installed Cubs general manager Andy McPhail tapped Riggleman to lead the Cubs.

His first three seasons in Chicago, the Cubs continued to lose. But in 1998, things jelled. The front office acquired several veteran players and Riggleman got superb pitching from Kevin Tapani and rookie Kerry Wood. In addition, Sammy Sosa's home-run chase helped propel the club to 90 wins and a wild-card berth. But the Cubs lost three straight playoff games to the Atlanta Braves to end the season. In 1999, the Cubs resumed their losing ways, finishing last. Riggleman was fired at season's end.

Kevin Tapani
Pitcher, 1997 -

Pitcher Kevin Tapani was drafted by the Cubs in 1985, but didn't join the team until 12 years later.

Tapani decided to finish college rather than accept the Cubs' offer. By the time he signed with Chicago as a free agent in 1997, he had already pitched for four major-league teams.

His first year with the Cubs, Tapani started only 13 games because of surgery on his pitching hand. Still, he went 9-3. The next year, he won 19 games, a career year. In Game 2 of the playoffs against Atlanta, he took a 1-0 lead into the ninth inning before allowing a game-tying home run to Javy Lopez. The Cubs lost the game in 10 innings, 2-1.

Injuries cost Tapani two months of the 1999 season and he ended the year with only 6 wins. In 2000, he went 8-12, but suffered from an unreliable bullpen. Six times that season, he left the game with a lead, only to get a no-decision. He got off to a fast start in 2001, winning eight games by the All-Star break.

Henry Rodriguez
Outfielder, 1998-2000

In his first at bat with Chicago, slugger Henry Rodriguez hit a home run. By the time the season was over, he had hit 31 home runs and had driven in 85 runs.

Rodriguez's bat gave the Cubs a left-handed compliment to Sammy Sosa's. Together, the two outfielders hit 97 home runs in 1998, a single-season record for two Cubs teammates. From the outfield bleachers, fans took to throwing "O Henry" candy bars onto the grass to honor their new hero.

In 1999, Rodriguez batted .304 and hit 26 longballs, but he was not destined to stay in Chicago. In 2000, despite hitting 18 home runs and driving in 51 runs by late July, Rodriguez was traded to the Florida Marlins for two minor-leaguers.

Mickey Morandini
Infielder, 1998-1999

Mickey Morandini spent seven seasons with the Philadelphia Phillies before being traded to the Cubs after the 1997 season. The Cubs wanted a veteran second baseman to replace Ryne Sandberg and the price was rookie outfielder Doug Glanville.

His first season with the Cubs, Morandini had the best year of his career. He hit .296 with a career-high eight home runs and 53 RBI. He also led the league's second basemen in fielding percentage. But his average faded to .241 in 1999 and he was released at season's end. Morandini split the 2000 season between Toronto and Philadelphia.

Jose Hernandez
Infielder, 1994-1999

Jose Hernandez was a versatile glove man who played a variety of positions for the Cubs.

Hernandez split time between shortstop and third base, but secured a starting role in 1995 by hitting 13 home runs and driving in 40 runs in 93 games. The next year, however, Hernandez committed 20 errors and his batting average dropped. In 1997, he was used mostly as a late-inning reserve, although he often was called upon to pinch hit. In 1998, Hernandez came back to have a career year, hitting 23 home runs and driving in 75 runs to help put the Cubs in the playoffs.

Hernandez was traded to the Atlanta Braves along with pitcher Terry Mulholland at the trading deadline in 1999. He signed with the Milwaukee Brewers for the 2000 season.

Terry Mulholland
Pitcher, 1997-1999

Pitcher Terry Mulholland was another of the veterans who helped the Cubs win the 1998 wildcard spot.

Mulholland came to the Cubs after playing for four other clubs. The Cubs used him as a starter initially, but moved him to the bullpen in 1998, where he blossomed into the team's most reliable set-up man. Mulholland's rubber arm allowed manager Jim Riggleman to look to him when the Cubs needed a couple of extra innings. Mulholland appeared in 70 games and had a sparkling 2.89 ERA.

In 1999, Mulholland went 6-6 before being dealt to the Altanta Braves at the trading deadline. In Atlanta, he alternated between the bullpen and a starter's role. He signed with Pittsburgh as a free agent for 2001, but missed most of the season because of injuries.

Gary Gaetti
Third baseman, 1998-1999

Gary Gaetti's clutch hitting in the final six weeks of the 1998 season helped propel the Cubs to the postseason.

Gaetti arrived from St. Louis late in the season and was a powerful addition down the stretch. In the final 37 games, he batted .320, with eight home runs and 27 RBI. And in the one-game playoff against the Giants, his two-run homer secured a 5-3 Cubs victory, clinching the wild-card slot.

But it was a last hurrah for Gaetti, 40. The following season, he hit only .204. The Cubs released him after the 1999 season. Gaetti played five more games for the Boston Red Sox before retiring.

Kerry Wood
Wrigley Field, 1998

Cubs fans hadn't seen a pitching phenom like Kerry Lee Wood since Hall of Famer Ferguson Jenkins in the late 1960's. Like Jenkins, Wood piled up strikeouts in record numbers.

Wood, 20, came to the Cubs in 1998 after three years in the minors, where he had averaged better than a strike-out an inning. The Cubs made him the fourth overall pick in the 1995 draft right out of high school. He patterned himself after another fellow Texan, Nolan Ryan.

On May 6, in his fifth major-league start against the Houston Astros at Wrigley Field, Wood pitched a game that rewrote the record books. He struck out the first five batters he faced. Only a single by Astros shortstop Ricky Gutierrez in the third inning prevented Wood from tossing a no-hitter. Before a stunned crowd of almost 16,000, Wood struck out 20 batters that day, setting a new National League single-game record and tying the all-time major-league mark set by Roger Clemens. For Wood, the game started a streak of fanning 10 or more batters nine times that year.

For the season, Wood struck out 233 batters in 166 innings. For his efforts, he became the first Cubs pitcher ever named National League Rookie of the Year.

Sammy Sosa and Mark McGwire
Busch Stadium, 1998

It had been 38 years since baseball fans last saw a home-run show like the one produced by the Cubs' Sammy Sosa and the Cardinals' Mark McGwire in the summer of 1998.

In 1961, Yankees teammates Mickey Mantle and Roger Maris captured the nation's fascination as they pursued Babe Ruth's record of 60 home runs in a season. Maris won the race and set a new record with 61 home runs, a number that stood unchallenged for almost four decades.

The climate changed in the summer of 1998. In June, Sosa hit 20 home runs, the most ever in a single month by any player. By the end of August, Sosa and McGwire both had hit 55 home runs and their home-run duel had become the talk of the country. The only question seemed to be who would reach 62 first. McGwire broke the tape, hitting number 62 off Cubs pitcher Steve Trachsel on September 8 in St. Louis. On September 25, both players hit number 66. It was the end of the line for Sosa. But in the last two games of the season, McGwire went on a tear and hit four more, finishing with an historic 70 home runs. For his part, Sosa was named the National League's most valuable player.

Mark Grace
Wrigley Field, 2000

During the 1990's, no player in the major leagues had more hits than Cubs first baseman Mark Grace. Nor did any player hit more doubles than he did. Grace hit 456 doubles with Chicago, the most by a Cubs player in the 20th century.

Grace was a model of consistency in the field and at the plate. He won four Gold Glove awards and is the Cubs' all-time leader in fielding percentage at first base. He hit over .300 in nine of 13 seasons and, with 2,201 hits, ranks fifth on the Cubs' all-time hit list.

For all that he gave Chicago, Grace was denied a chance to finish his career at Wrigley Field. When his contract was up after the 2000 season, the Cubs' front office didn't make him an offer. At age 36, Grace signed as a free agent with the Arizona Diamondbacks.

Kerry Wood
Pitcher, 1998 -

With a month to go in the 1998 season, Cubs' ace Kerry Wood damaged the ligaments in his right elbow and went on the disabled list, a stay that lasted more than a year. The loss was devastating to the Cubs, who lost 95 games in 1999 and finished last.

In 2000, Wood came back slowly and, while clearly not in full form, won eight games. In 2001, after losing four of his first five starts, Wood caught fire. By the All-Star break, he had won eight games and the Cubs found themselves in first place. Wood's bulldog mentality rubbed off on teammates, who jelled and played their most consistent ball in three seasons.

The future of the Cubs in the new century will be linked to the health and performance of players like Wood. The Cubs' faithful fans can only hope that decades of futility will soon be replaced by a championship banner flying over Wrigley Field.

Photograph Index

Photograph Credits

Blank, Steve:
28

Brace, George:
109, 127, 135, 136, 137, 138, 140, 143, 146(right), 156, 169(left)

Chicago Historical Society:
(Chicago Daily News negatives collection)
11 (SDN-00359)
19 (SDN-060449)
35 (SDN-058203)
41 (SDN-061544)
42 left (SDN-062504)

Chicago Sports Photographers:
161, 162, 164, 166, 167, 168, 169(right), 170, 171, 172, 173, 174, 175, 176, 177, 179, 181, 182, 183, 184, 185, 187, 189, 191, 192, 193, 194(left), 197, 198, 199(right), 200, 201, 202, 203, 207

Cincinnati Enquirer, The:
8, 9, 10, 26, 40, 57, 62, 79, 158

Cleveland State University:
(Cleveland Press archives)
27, 141

Goldstein, Dennis:
14, 18, 32(left), 37, 43, 51, 53(left), 55, 60(right), 64, 80, 92, 99, 117

Knoll, Dan:
frontispiece, 22, 24, 30, 33, 44, 52(left), 61, 71, 72, 73, 78, 85, 88(right), 93, 125, 144

Loughman, Bill:
45, 47, 52(right), 53(right), 54, 59, 69, 74, 75, 77, 83, 84, 89, 91, 96, 97, 101, 104, 105, 107, 108, 112, 113, 115, 120, 122, 131, 132, 163

McWilliams, Doug:
148, 149, 150(left), 151, 152, 153, 154, 155, 157, 159, 160

Mumby, Mike:
12, 17, 21, 29, 34(left), 42(right), 48, 49(left), 60(left), 65, 87

National Baseball Hall of Fame Library:
Cooperstown, NY
16, 23, 25, 31, 32(right), 34(right), 36, 38, 39, 50, 56, 58, 63, 66, 67, 76, 81, 82, 86, 88(left), 90, 94, 95, 98, 100, 102, 103, 106, 110, 111, 114, 116, 118, 124, 126, 129, 130, 146(left),

Sparks, Don:
128, 147

Stang, Mark:
68

The Sporting News:
13, 15, 20, 70, 119, 121, 123, 133, 139, 142, 145, 150(right), 165, 178, 180, 186, 188, 190

Transcendental Graphics:
46, 49(right), 134

Trombetti, Skip:
194(right), 195, 196, 199(left)

Harry Caray
Wrigley Field

Broadcaster Harry Caray signs autographs before a game at Wrigley Field.
Caray's legacy lives on at the corner of Clark and Addison through the voice of
his grandson, Chip, who has been behind the Cubs' microphone since 1998.

To order additional copies of *Cubs Collection*, or for information about other titles currently available from Orange Frazer Press, please call **1–800–852–9332**, or visit our website at **orangefrazer.com**. Address inquiries to:
Orange Frazer Press
P.O. Box 214
37½ West Main Street
Wilmington, OH 45177.